WRITING ILLINOIS

WRITING ILLINOIS

The Prairie, Lincoln, and Chicago

JAMES HURT

UNIVERSITY OF ILLINOIS PRESS
Urbana and Chicago

Publication of this book is supported in part by a grant from the Research Board of the University of Illinois at Urbana-Champaign.

This book is printed on acid-free paper.

Library of Congress Cataloging-in-Publication Data

Hurt, James, 1934–
    Writing Illinois : the prairie, Lincoln, and Chicago / James Hurt.
        p.   cm.
    Includes bibliographical references and index.
    ISBN 0-252-01850-8 (alk. paper)
    1. American literature—Illinois—History and criticism.
  2. Lincoln, Abraham, 1809–1865, in fiction, drama, poetry, etc.
  3. Chicago (Ill.) in literature.   4. Illinois—Intellectual life.
  5. Illinois in literature.   6. Prairies in literature.   I. Title.
    PS283.I3H87   1992
  810.9′32773—dc20   91-14346
                                                       CIP

Contents

Acknowledgments

I began writing *Writing Illinois* during a sabbatical leave and an appointment at the University of Illinois Center for Advanced Study in 1986–87. Thanks are due to both the University and the Center for the unencumbered time. A revised version was completed in Dublin, Ireland, where I taught as an exchange professor at St. Patrick's College during 1987–88. My hosts in the English Department at St. Pat's made me very welcome and were always ready to hear about the prairie, Lincoln, and Chicago, often over a pint: Pat Burke, Brenna Clarke, Michael Clarke, Tom Halpin, Celia Keenan, and John Killeen. Celia Keenan, Martin Maguire, Nora Maguire, and Betty Maguire helped in more ways than I can say. Back home in Illinois, Zohreh Sullivan, Bruce Michelson, Robert Bray, and an anonymous reader for the University of Illinois Press devoted immense amounts of time to detailed critiques of the manuscript, which benefited accordingly. Carol Severins, Marlyn Ehlers, and Rene Wahlfeldt saved my bacon several times when word-processing Illinois threatened to defeat me. Richard Wentworth and Jane Mohraz have been dream editors, Dick for his long-sustained faith in the book, Jane for both her interest in the book, generally, and her killer pencil, specifically.

Introduction

Writing Illinois emerged from a simple impulse to understand better the place where, though not a native, I have lived and worked for the past quarter-century. I am especially interested in a phenomenon I think my ears have become especially attuned to during that time: a curious sort of ambivalence in the way my fellow Illinoisans talk about where they live, a mixture of affection and embarrassment. It usually takes a humorous form, in jokes about the flatness of the landscape, the provinciality of the culture, the ugliness of Chicago. (Peoria jokes alone are a major genre of Illinois popular culture.) Or it can take the form of a hollow boosterism, in phrases like "the breadbasket of the world," "the city that works," or "the heartland," phrases that betray a nervous defensiveness as much as anything else.

It could be argued that humorous self-deprecation and cultural insecurity are part of a midwestern style and are not peculiar to Illinois. James M. Cox, in a recent essay on regionalism in American literature, has explored the roots of the estrangement that midwesterners (or midwestern writers, at any rate) have felt from their environment. He defines the Midwest as "a region true to its geographical designation: a middle west absolutely occupied and defined by the middle class" (773). Arguing from the examples of Theodore Dreiser, Gertrude Stein, Sherwood Anderson, T. S. Eliot, Sinclair Lewis, Ernest Hemingway, Ring Lardner, F. Scott Fitzgerald, and Willa Cather—midwesterners all—Cox finds the "true emotion of middle-class, Middle Western writers" to be "estrangement from the flat landscapes, towns, and society on which they looked" (774).[1]

It is hard to argue with Cox's description of a white-bread, white-boy Midwest, given the list of authors he takes as definitive of midwestern culture; the flight from the physical and spiritual flatness of prairie and village is, it cannot be denied, a recurring action in midwestern writing. I would suggest two qualifications though.

First, I wonder what would happen if that all-important qualifier "middle-class" were removed from Cox's list. Removing it would allow us to include Richard Wright as well as Ernest Hemingway, Carl Sandburg as well as T. S. Eliot, Gwendolyn Brooks as well as Gertrude Stein, Vachel Lindsay as well as Sinclair Lewis. The note of estrangement is heard in some of these marginalized voices, too, though it is not always estrangement merely from artistically barren environments, and notes of affirmation and even celebration are heard in others. Cox's traditional view of midwestern literature operates by exclusion and is, to that extent, partial. The Midwest is more culturally pluralistic than he allows for, and William Cullen Bryant's prairies, Sandburg's Lincoln, and Cyrus Colter's, Nelson Algren's, and Saul Bellow's Chicagos have contributed to our sense of place in the Midwest, as much as the works of such displaced midwesterners as Eliot and Hemingway have.

Second, I wonder if anything could be learned from making nicer discriminations than "midwestern"? Granted that certain themes recur in midwestern literature ("estrangement from flatness," perhaps), may not those themes find distinctive expressions in different parts of the Midwest, be shaped by different available mythologies, be affected by the experience of different ethnic groups and subcultures? Just as we do not allow the category "southern literature" to obscure the difference between, say, Mississippi and New Orleans, so we should not flatten out the Midwest into an undifferentiated mass.

As we look at it, Cox's definition of midwestern literature comes to seem more a definition of the literature between 1900 and 1950 of white, largely male, middle-class expatriates from a large, undifferentiated land mass in the middle of the continent. If we broaden our range of writers by dropping our canonical gates and narrow

---

1. Illinois's "middleness" is well described in Cullom Davis's fine essay on Illinois.

our geographical coverage to Illinois in the interest of specificity and concreteness, we may arrive at conclusions somewhat different from Cox's.

So Illinois, from the beginning to the present. But why the prairie, Lincoln, and Chicago? Why organize the material by subject matter rather than by chronology, author, or genre—much more familiar choices? The topical organization is intended to throw the emphasis on cultural construction, the sort of world we have written for ourselves and the way we have written ourselves into it. The more Illinois texts I read, the more I become aware of how much the sense of place in Illinois has been formed around the fact of the prairie landscape, the memory of Lincoln, and the presence of Chicago. The three are intertwined: the prairie is recurringly represented as embodied in Lincoln; Lincoln is depicted as either the inevitable or the inexplicable product of the prairie; and Chicago is seen in prairie terms, as either a blasphemous inversion or a natural extension of it.

As I read and reread the literatures of the prairie, Lincoln, and Chicago, it also occurs to me that there are certain parallels among them. In one form or another, the idea recurs of making something out of nothing. The first white travelers stood on the edge of the Grand Prairie, surveyed its vast emptiness, and asked if such a void could ever support a civilization. The earliest biographers of Lincoln, and later ones as well, looked at his frontier background and wondered, with William Herndon, who knew that background firsthand, how such a man could have risen from such "a stagnant, putrid pool" (9)—such nothingness. When Saul Bellow's Charlie Citrine, in *Humboldt's Gift,* surveys a desolate landscape and says, "I was trained in Chicago to make something of such a scant setting. In Chicago you become a connoisseur of the near-nothing" (23), he is echoing a century of Chicago description that found it an extravagant civilization built on a cultural void.

Looked at a slightly different way, "nothingness" is simply the new. Prairie travelers saw nothing in the landscape because they saw nothing familiar. Lincoln's contemporaries saw him as springing from nothing because they could recognize none of the traditional ways of preparing for leadership in his frontier background. Observers of Chicago looked at a new urban culture and found it a void because it did not resemble traditional cultures; some of the greatest achievements of Chicago architecture, for example, were for a long time not acknowledged to be architecture at all, because they did not resemble European buildings.

In a sense, this experience is the exemplary American one. To white Europeans, all America was once new, a blank slate of nothingness upon which they could write their desire. In Illinois the encounter with nothing and the attempt to make something out of it took its own form. The East Coast, with its forests, streams, and rolling hills, was close enough to European landscapes to be read in European terms. The Illinois prairie was the first landscape encountered as the frontier moved west that completely resisted assimilation to European precedents; the closest analogy was the Russian steppes, to which they were occasionally rather desperately compared. Lincoln, too, was read even by his contemporaries, such as Ralph Waldo Emerson, as something unprecedented: the first prominent American to have risen from wholly American roots. Chicago, with its frighteningly rapid growth after the Great Fire of 1871, was by the end of the century first among modern cities, a new phenomenon that also could not be read in traditional languages.

Perhaps because the prairie, Lincoln, and Chicago were all initially perceived as unprecedented, versions of the American Other, all three have been at various times the subjects of heated debate. The Illinois prairie was the subject of sharp controversy during the period of settlement, particularly in the flood of books and pamphlets inspired by the founding of the English Prairie in Edwards County. The combatants in this paper war tended to represent the Illinois prairie either as an Edenic garden or as a barren, pestilential desert. Sometimes the contradiction merely reflected a disagreement over the prospects for successful settlement. But often, even in the most mundane texts, the topic of the prairie seemed to open up deeper cultural anxieties over the possibility of constructing a viable culture in such emptiness. In my first chapter, I begin by sampling the voluminous literature of prairie description by early travelers and settlers and the ways they attempt to find meaning in the prairie. I then follow these interpretations into their expression in William Cullen Bryant's well-known poem "The Prairies" and end with extended discussions of three book-length narratives of the Illinois prairie: Eliza Farnham's *Life in Prairie Land,* John Regan's *Emigrant's Guide to the Western States of America,* and Francis Grierson's *Valley of Shadows.*

The figure of Lincoln stands at the center of a civil war of cultural conflicts that reach to the roots of American life, and the unabating flood of Lincoln discourse is more a symptom of irresolution than a movement toward resolution. The cultural energies invested in the symbolic Lincoln are suggested by the remarkable storm of praise and abuse that broke over the publication in 1984 of Gore Vidal's witty and ironic (and serious) *Lincoln: A Novel,* an attempt to provide a Lincoln for grown-ups. I begin chapter 2 with an analysis of this tempest in a teapot, with a view to opening up some issues in the representation of Lincoln by distinguishing between realist and nominalist positions and suggesting that the familiar polarization of "myth" and "reality" is not a very useful way to understand Lincoln texts. I then move to a study of the representation of Lincoln in Herndon's biography, Jane Addams's *Twenty Years at Hull-House,* and the Lincoln poems of Vachel Lindsay, Edgar Lee Masters, and Carl Sandburg and end with an extended analysis of Sandburg's *Abraham Lincoln: The Prairie Years and the War Years.*

Chicago, as cultural symbol, is as riddled with conflicts as the prairie and Lincoln are, and these conflicts have centered on similar issues: whether its civilization is a brave, new American one or no civilization at all. The canonical account of Chicago literature represents it as brutally naturalistic, presenting the city as a jungle of male conflict ending in the defeat of the individual. I begin chapter 3 with a critique of this traditional narrativization of Chicago's literary history, suggesting that it rests on a very narrow range of texts and surveying evidence that complicates and enriches the received account. The major portion of the chapter, however, is given over to a study of the representation of Chicago in the literature of the city of the last forty years, a topic generally omitted in the standard histories. I begin with a comparison of Nelson Algren's *Chicago: City on the Make* and Studs Terkel's *Chicago,* move on to works by Cyrus Colter, Maxine Chernoff, Stuart Dybek, and Paul Hoover, and end with an extended study of the meaning of Chicago in the fiction of Saul Bellow. The book thus has a loosely chronological structure as well as a topical one, beginning with nineteenth-century accounts of the prairie, continuing with accounts of Lincoln from 1889 to 1944, and concluding with accounts of Chicago from 1951 to 1990.

The idea of making something out of nothing as the exemplary Illinois gesture may help explain the cultural uncertainty I noted initially, the tendency to give with one hand and take away with the other when we describe our home country. We are still unsure about what we have created on those vast prairies, about what Lincoln means, about how Chicago stacks up to New York or London: we are still trying to make something out of nothing. The prairie, Lincoln, and Chicago as literal features of Illinois history have become "the prairie," "Lincoln," and "Chicago" as they have been incorporated into culture and have become encrusted with interpretations upon interpretations. The interpretations will continue as writers continue to reflect on what we have created out of all this emptiness.

1

Writing the Prairie

The Prairie Travelers

In 1833, a young Scotsman named Patrick Shirreff visited Illinois in the course of an American tour undertaken so he could advise his younger brother about emigration. He rode out of the village of Chicago southwest toward Springfield and within a few miles had his first glimpse of an Illinois prairie. His description contains such a concentration of the leading motifs of prairie description as to merit quoting at some length:

> Having reached Chicago with an unsocial party of travellers, and gradually passing from the forests and oak openings of Michigan, it was not until after crossing the river Des Plaines that I became fully sensible of the beauty and sublimity of the prairies. They embrace every texture of soil and outline of surface, and are sufficiently undulating to prevent the stagnation of water. The herbage consists of tall grass, interspersed with flowering plants of every hue, which succeed each other as the season advances. The blossoming period was nearly over at the time of my journey. Sunflowers were particularly numerous, and almost all the plants had yellow blossoms. Every day brought me in contact with species formerly unobserved, while others with which I had become familiar, disappeared. Occasionally, clumps of trees stood out on the surface, like islands in the ocean. The bounding forest projected and receded in pleasing forms, and the distant outlines appeared graceful. I had no time for searching out and studying scenery, and perhaps conceptions of beauty and grouping of trees, formed in the artificial school of Britain, are inapplicable to the magnificent scale on which nature hath adorned the

country between Chicago and Springfield. The works of man are mere distortions compared with those of nature, and I have no doubt many prairies, containing hundreds of square miles, exceed the finest English parks in beauty as much as they do in extent. Sometimes I found myself in the midst of the area without a tree or object of any kind within the range of vision, the surface, clothed with interesting vegetation around me, appearing like a sea, suggested ideas which I had not then the means of recording, and cannot be recalled. The wide expanse appeared the gift of God to man for the exercise of his industry; and there being no obstacle to immediate cultivation, nature seemed inviting the husbandman to till the soil, and partake of her bounty. (quoted in Angle 132–33)

I have begun with Shirreff's description not because it is distinguished writing but because of its typicality of a motif that recurs in practically every traveler's account of early Illinois, a motif so common that it constitutes almost a topos of western travel writing: the First View of the Prairie.[1] By the 1830s, the prairies had been described so often that prairie passages had taken on a rather formulaic quality, following conventions of Romantic picturesque travel writing, adapted to a novel landscape. It is hard to believe that Shirreff had not read earlier descriptions, so strong is the sense in the passage that he is trying to live up to expectations, including "searching out and studying scenery" and producing sublime thoughts (which he rather lamely insists he had but has since forgotten).[2]

---

1. Shock and protestations of indescribability on first encountering unfamiliar landscapes are common all over the world, not just on the Illinois prairie. Roy Campbell has parodied similar accounts of the South African veldt: "There is something grander, yes, / About the veldt, than I can well express, / Something more vast— perhaps I don't mean that— / Something more round, and square, and steep, and flat . . . / Something more 'nameless'—That's the very word!" (25).

2. Indispensable in the study of prairie literature are Ralph Leslie Rusk's *The Literature of the Middle Western Frontier* and Dorothy Anne Dondore's *The Prairie and the Making of Middle America*. An excellent study of the prairie in literature is Steven Douglas Olson's "Metaphor of the Prairie in Nineteenth-Century American Poetry." Robert Thacker's *Great Prairie Fact and Literary Imagination* is a comprehensive study. Thacker's definition of the prairie is very broad: "that area of generally level unforested farmland—formerly grassland—between the Ohio River and the plateaus of the West that extends north into Canada to include portions of the provinces of Manitoba, Saskatchewan, and Alberta, and south to include the area extending to the gulf coast of Texas" (6). This breadth is both a strength, in that it suggests similarities of response to flatness, and a limitation, in that it obscures the special interpretation of the prairie at any particular historical moment.

Shirreff organizes his description loosely along the lines of picturesque painting and landscape description, dividing the scene into foreground (the "interesting vegetation around me"), middle ground (the islandlike clumps of trees), and background (the "distant outlines" of the "bounding forest"). He invokes the almost obligatory comparison to the ocean, along with the comparison of the groves of trees to islands, and the almost equally common comparison of the landscape to a cultivated English park, with the conventional insistence that the works of nature exceed those of man. Despite Shirreff's reference to the "beauty and sublimity" of the prairies, he emphasizes the beauty rather than the sublimity; he seeks picturesque irregularity and variety in the monotonous landscape and humanizes the scene with a conventional flower passage. He ends by feminizing the landscape in a perhaps unconscious sexual metaphor in which nature invites the "husbandman" to till her soil and partake of her bounty.

Despite the conventional elements in his description, the passage conveys a strong sense of Shirreff's mind at work, struggling to find terms to contain a powerful experience and falling back, sometimes rather clumsily, on conventions earlier travelers had used to represent the same experience. It is perhaps not too fanciful to see an act of cultural colonization going on in the passage. As in many such descriptions, a solitary horseman rides into the immense emptiness of the prairie and organizes it with his gaze along lines that connect it with the familiar: the ocean, the "finest English parks," even a sexually available female. Such conceptualizing makes the conclusion possible: the prairie is "the gift of God to man for the exercise of his industry."

Shirreff aestheticizes the prairie along conventional lines, but his evocation of the beauty of the prairie and the conventions he draws on to do so are not purely aesthetic. Landscape description along these lines serves certain cultural needs both for Shirreff and for his predecessors. Faced with a vast, empty, monotonous landscape, Shirreff draws on picturesque aesthetics to rationalize settlement, finding enough variety in the landscape to allow drainage, regarding the immense distances and the isolation as an instance of divine sublimity rather than hindrances to settlement, and representing the relationship between settler and land as reenacting fantasized gender roles.

By no means all descriptions of the Illinois prairie were as romantically affirmative as Shirreff's. The negative features of the prairie repressed by his picturesque treatment often became the dominant theme in a large body of antiemigration literature. The most famous of these negative descriptions is by Charles Dickens in *American Notes* (1842), a passage vastly elaborated in *Martin Chuzzlewit*. He is describing his first view of Looking-Glass Prairie, near St. Louis:

> This course decided on, and the horses being well refreshed, we again pushed forward, and came upon the Prairie at sunset. It would be difficult to say why, or how—though it was possibly from having heard and read so much about it—but the effect on me was disappointment. Looking towards the setting sun, there lay, stretched out before my view, a vast expanse of level ground; unbroken, save by one thin line of trees, which scarcely amounted to a scratch upon the great blank; until it met the glowing sky, wherein it seemed to dip; mingling with its rich colours, and mellowing in its distant blue. There it lay, a tranquil sea or lake without water, if such a simile be admissible, with the day going down upon it; a few birds wheeling here and there; and solitude and silence reigning paramount around. But the grass was not yet high; there were bare black patches on the ground; and the few wild flowers that the eye could see, were poor and scanty. Great as the picture was, its very flatness and extent, which left nothing to the imagination, tamed it down and cramped its interest. I felt little of that sense of freedom and exhilaration which a Scottish heath inspires, or even our English downs awaken. I felt that in traversing the Prairies I could never abandon myself to the scene, forgetful of all else; as I should do instinctively, were the heather underneath my feet, or an iron-bound coast beyond; but should often glance toward a distant and frequently-receding line of the horizon, and wish it gained and passed. It is not a scene to be forgotten, but it is scarcely one, I think (at all events, as I saw it), to remember with much pleasure, or to covet the looking-on again, in after life. (quoted in Angle 209–10)

This is an extraordinarily subtle and sensitive passage, which translates into terms of landscape description not only a recurring theme of Dickens's criticism of American life but also a familiar theme in responses to the prairie. Dickens's First View of the Prairie is as conventionalized in structure as Shirreff's; he has obviously, as he says, read about the prairie, and he includes his own versions of the invocation of the sea, the distant trees bounding the prairie's expanse, and even a flower passage (or an antiflower passage, noting the "poor and scanty" wild flowers). Like Shirreff, he aestheticizes the prairie, regarding the scene as "a picture," though he finds the picture disappointing. But his description of the prairie differs from Shirreff's not only in the very different conclusions he draws but also in his self-consciousness about the problem of description; his description is as much about the process of description as it is about the prairie itself. It is "difficult to say why, or how" he was disappointed, he says, and he explores the source of the difficulty throughout the passage. Behind the movement of his thought, we can sense a sublime representation of the prairie that is being examined and tested. The scene does have a sublime vastness, silence, and richness of color where the far-off horizon meets the sky. Although the scale is greater than that of a Scottish heath or the English downs, the effect is paradoxically tamer and more cramped. Dickens would feel more freedom and exhilaration if he could sense boundaries around the landscape, even if he could not see them— an "iron-bound coast" invisibly enclosing the scene.

Dickens's prairie description is no more culturally neutral than Shirreff's. The aesthetics of sublimity are being placed at the service of cultural criticism, here a thoughtful and ironic consideration of the claims of American freedom against English restraint. Dickens's paradoxical uses of the imagery of freedom and enclosure repeat themes throughout *American Notes* and *Martin Chuzzlewit*. The "iron-bound coast," confining and limiting the freedom of the heath and downs, suggests a limiting and yet reassuringly stable social order, within which the individual can seek personal freedom. But what if there is nothing but freedom, a complete openness of Edenic possibility? The prospect deeply disturbs Dickens, as it did a number of American writer-travelers to the West.

If Shirreff and Dickens were representative in some ways of early writer-travelers to Illinois, they were of course far from representative of the mass of settlers who poured into the Illinois country in the first half of the nineteenth century. Well-educated, literate, and British, Shirreff and Dickens obviously brought preconceptions and expectations to their encounter with the Illinois prairie that would have been very foreign to the majority of immigrants to Illinois, who were more likely to be poor, uneducated, and American and more likely to look for water and wood than for beauty and sublimity in their surroundings. A glance at the writers included in a collection such as Paul Angle's *Prairie State: Impressions of Illinois, 1673–1967, by Travelers and Other Observers* is enough to demonstrate the gap between those who settled the state and those who wrote about it. A disproportionate number of Angle's writers were British, and a large number of them were, like Dickens, professional writers. As a matter of fact, many of the early descriptions of Illinois were written by people who visited Illinois only to write a book about it.

Nevertheless, it is in the work of this unrepresentative group that the Illinois prairie entered the American imagination: history is the creation of those who write the books. Shirreff and Dickens were typical of these writer-travelers in the Romantic preconceptions they brought to their experiences. Like most of their contemporaries, they were picturesque travelers, predisposed to see the country-side as a series of pictures or prospects that could be measured against standards of beauty and sublimity. As they gazed on the new landscapes before them, they consulted their own responses, seeking a vital correspondence between external nature and their own consciousnesses. The Illinois prairie, like most of the American landscape, thus entered public discourse in Romantic terms, in the language of the sublime, the beautiful, and the picturesque, with cultural issues expressed in pervasively aesthetic terms.

The English Prairie

Opposing views of the prairie and the cultural assumptions and conflicts underlying them are most fully represented in the voluminous literature of the English Prairie, the English community founded in 1817 by Morris Birkbeck and George Flower in Edwards County in southern Illinois.[3] At least twenty-eight books dealing exclusively or in large part with the English Prairie flowed out of English and American presses between 1817 and 1836. Birkbeck himself was responsible for four of them: *Notes on a Journey in America* (1817), *Letters from Illinois* (1818), *Extracts from a Supplementary Letter from the Illinois* (1819), and *An Address to the Farmers of Great Britain* (1822), books so seductive in the promises they held out to emigrants that a contemporary wrote, "No man, since

---

3. For a history of the English Prairie largely told in the words of those involved, see Charles Boewe, *Prairie Albion.*

Columbus, has done so much toward peopling America as Mr. Birk-beck, whose publications, and the authority of whose name, had effects truly prodigious" (Faux 298). Apart from a pamphlet or two, Flower did not contribute to the literature of the English Prairie until 1860, when he was an old man. Forced by financial reverses to leave the town he had founded, in ill health, and operating an inn in Mount Vernon, Indiana, he turned his thoughts back half a century and wrote *History of the English Settlement in Edwards County, Illinois.* Meanwhile, however, Birkbeck's promotional materials for the settlement had called forth a storm of controversy, beginning with the acidulous William Cobbett, who in an 1819 open letter to Birkbeck told him that "a warm heart, a lively imagination, and I know not what republicanism" had led him into a wild "Transallega-nian dream," and that "your books, written, I am sure, without any intention to deceive and decoy, are, in my opinion, calculated to produce great disappointment, not to say misery and ruin, amongst our own country people" (332). The issue thus stated, over the next fifteen years or so almost everyone who wrote about the western settlements—Henry Bradshaw Fearon, William Faux, William Blane, William Tell Harris, and a host of others—felt it incumbent upon himself or herself to visit the English Prairie and pronounce on the reality behind Birkbeck's honeyed words.

The controversy over the English Prairie involved whether Birk-beck had fairly represented the prospects for immigrants to the settlement, but underlying this disagreement was a more basic conflict of political principles. Birkbeck was not a revolutionary by any means and the English Prairie was not designed to be a radical utopian community like New Harmony, Indiana. As he makes clear in his books, however, Birkbeck left England in protest against the repressive measures that followed the French Revolution, and he planned the English Prairie as a community where everyone could own land, vote, and exercise complete freedom of religion. These principles angered his antagonists far more than any deceptive advertising he might have engaged in did. The reactionary *Quarterly Review,* for example, devoted twenty-five pages to a review of *Notes on a Journey in America* in the same volume in which it attacked Keats's *Endymion,* and it aimed directly at Birkbeck's libertarian notions. "Whatever 'New America' may have gained by the name of Birkbeck having ceased to be found in the list of the citizens of Old

England, the latter have no reason to regret the loss," the reviewer wrote. "Many more of the same stamp may well be spared to wage war with the bears and Red Indians of the 'backwoods' of America" (quoted in Thomson 33).

These political differences color the lenses through which observers saw the English Prairie, whether as a democratic garden or a bog for the swinish multitude. Here, for example, is George Flower's First View of Boltenhouse Prairie, the site of the English settlement:

> A few steps more, and a beautiful prairie suddenly opened to our view. At first, we only received the impressions of its general beauty. With longer gaze, all its distinctive features were revealed, lying in profound repose under the warm light of an afternoon's summer sun. Its indented and irregular outline of wood, its varied surface interspersed with clumps of oaks of centuries' growth, its tall grass, with seed stalks from six to ten feet high, like tall and slender reeds waving in a gentle breeze, the whole presenting a magnificence of park-scenery, complete from the hand of Nature, and unrivalled by the same sort of scenery by European art. For once, reality came up to the picture of imagination. (64)

This passage is only one of many prairie descriptions in Flower's book, a Romantic celebration of the interaction of the individual and nature. Here is another, which appears soon after the description of Boltenhouse Prairie:

> One small prairie charmed me very much—not more than two hundred yards wide and about half-a-mile long. A thin belt of tall and graceful trees marked its boundary from other and larger prairies. Its distinguishing feature was a large Indian mound in the centre, covered with the same rank growth of grass as in other parts of the prairie. Its beauties lying in silent solitude, with its ancient burial-place of a by-gone race, gave to it an unusual and somewhat mysterious interest. These tumuli are not the burying-place of the present race of Indians; but of an anterior race, probably displaced by the Indians as we are displacing them. (71)

These passages demonstrate, perhaps even more than the one from Shirreff, the naturalizing function of the conventions of prairie description, the way a strange and potentially forbidding landscape is domesticated by being connected to desirable familiar landscapes, both natural and derived from picturesque painting. The landscape is perceived as "park-scenery," painted by nature as artist, and is "unrivalled by the same sort of scenery by European art." (In Flower's day, a *park* was the ornamental tract surrounding a country house or mansion, rather than a deliberately preserved piece of nature, as in more modern meanings of the word. Its connotations thus had more to do with culture than with nature. See the *Oxford English Dictionary*.) In the second passage, Flower introduces a motif that was to recur frequently in prairie description, Indian burial mounds. Here, as in many other descriptions, the mounds reflect several cultural needs. Aesthetically, the mounds supply the place of ruins in picturesque landscapes, humanizing the scene, providing a sense of historical depth, and giving it, in Flower's words, "an unusual and somewhat mysterious interest." Interpreted as relics of a race that preceded the contemporary Indians, the mounds also are incorporated into the ideology of settlement. If the Indians displaced a previous race, then their title to the land is no more legitimate than that of the white settlers, and white settlement can be seen as merely part of a natural cycle of rise and decline. If the "mound-builders" were thought to be a white race—a point Flower does not make, but his contemporaries often did—then the rationalization also contains rather disturbing racial overtones.[4]

That Flower's prairie descriptions are not merely ornamental touches but represent an intensely Romantic and deeply felt view of settlement is made clear by his *History of the English Settlement,* in which, despite many disappointments and reversals, he never questions the wisdom of emigrating as he did. The first settler, he says late in the book, "pierces through civilization, and stands in uninhabited regions."

> There he sees what none who come after him and fall into the routine of civilized life can ever see; nature in the plenitude of its perfection; its varied beauties, undisturbed and undistorted by art; the forest in its native grandeur, unscathed by the axe; the prairie, with its verdure and acres of brilliant flowers; the beauties of the prospect varying at every step, and limited in extent only by his power of vision. All these scenes, with their accompanying influences, exhibited under the varying aspects of light and shade, day and night, calm and storm, have surrounded him. His being has received the impress of them all in solitude and silence. Re-

---

4. On the myth of the mound-builders, see Robert Silverberg, *Mound Builders of Ancient America*.

freshed, strengthened, and purified, he feels, for a time at least, superior to the irritations and annoyances of an imperfect civilization; for there is in the changeful heart of man a deep response to the ever-changing aspects of nature. (357)

Flower's Romantic representation of the English Prairie, in which nature functions as tutulary spirit blessing the act of settlement, did not stand unchallenged. Birkbeck's and Flower's chief opponent in the paper war over the English Prairie was William Cobbett, who, in his *Year's Residence in the United States of America* (1819), vehemently attacked Birkbeck's claims for the settlement. Since Cobbett never visited Albion, however, he included no physical descriptions of the prairie. Close behind Cobbett in attacks on the settlement was William Faux, who did include a long negative account of the English Prairie in his eccentric *Memorable Days in America* (1823). This passage accurately represents Faux's gossipy, slightly spiteful tone:

> This family (the Flowers) own a large and beautiful domain of prairie, containing unnumbered acres of fine land, beautified by British park scenery. The visitor, coming here out of the forest, fancies himself in England, especially if he looks at the country through the windows of Messrs. Flower's and Birkbeck's houses, during the green and flowery season, when the scenery presents a wide waste of grass, flowers, and shrubs, of every hue; but the flowers have no fragrance, the birds no song. The sight of a flock of 500 Merino sheep, and a large herd of cattle, all their own, is indeed a novel and unexpected pleasure in these wild regions; and, added to all these, the comfort of such houses and harmonious families, escaped from the embarrassments and anxieties of England, to quiet rest and independence, makes it indeed a delightful spectacle. All say they have nothing to regret, and are full of satisfaction, except the wish that more friends would follow; whom, unless they follow, they shall see no more. They acknowledge that they have much to do here, from want of servants. One female, Biddy by name, recently came and engaged to do only what she pleased, and to sit at the same table. The terms were complied with, but a plan to cure Biddy was laid. On a certain day many visitors were invited to dinner, at which Biddy was not allowed to rise, even to help herself to any thing, but all present vied with each other in attending on Miss Biddy, who, in great confusion, left the room, fully sensible of her folly, and next day determined to be a servant for the future. (271–72)

Reuben Gold Thwaites, Faux's modern editor, notes Faux's "lack of manners and good taste, a coarse betrayal of hospitality, and a low-bred craving for notoriety," as well as his lack of organization and tendency to jump from one subject to another without transition (11–12). But the extraordinary combination of ideas in his bit of prairie description is perhaps more than just clumsiness; the association of ideas is significant, if not particularly logical.

Faux's English Prairie is a phantom landscape. He acknowledges its beauty and notes its similarity to an English park. But, he says, it is a "waste" in which "the flowers have no fragrance, the birds no song" (271). (A little later he describes the hay made from prairie grass as equally illusory; it appears "green and fragrant" but offers no nourishment [275].) The explanation for this curious description of the prairie, in which even nature seems unreal, perhaps appears in the story of Biddy, with which Faux, by an odd association of ideas, completes the paragraph. The point of this unpleasant little story about the humiliation of a presumptuous servant is the confirmation of social order. By refusing to stay in her place, Biddy threatens social hierarchy; her superiors conspire to correct her by acting out the consequences of such anarchy. There is a happy ending: Biddy becomes "fully sensible of her folly," resumes her place as a servant, and the social order is upheld. This structure, however, is missing in the larger community of the English settlement, as Faux makes clear in his descriptions of lawless rowdies, lazy workmen, and immigrants who have regressed into barbarism. The land lacks fences, both literal and metaphorical, and without literal fences to contain the livestock and social fences to contain the people, the prairie, beautiful as it appears, is useless.

A hundred and fifty years later, to read the literature inspired by the English Prairie is to recover a moment in Illinois history. The most immediate rewards are the views of the Illinois landscape on the eve of settlement: the breathtaking empty spaces, the towering prairie grass, the violent prairie storms, and the spectacular prairie fires that raced over the landscape each fall. The observers are even more interesting than what they observe, as they grope for words, metaphors, and analogies to translate their experiences into language their readers can connect with their own experiences. Behind these struggles to write the Illinois landscape lie cultural struggles over the meaning of freedom, the necessity for law, and exhilaration and fear over the prospective society that might evolve in such a place, one that might dissolve social hierarchies and produce a world turned upside down.

William Cullen Bryant's "The Prairies"

Descriptions of the Illinois prairie, with their implicit expressions of cultural conflict, culminate in a sensitive and troubling poem that distills many of the issues underlying earlier prairie descriptions: William Cullen Bryant's "The Prairies" (1833). Bryant first saw Illinois in 1832, when he went to visit two of his brothers who had settled in Jacksonville. "The Prairies" is a product of this visit.

An extended poetic treatment of the First View of the Prairies topos, "The Prairies" consists of four long, blank-verse paragraphs (see his *Poems,* 118–21). It begins with a description of the prairies:

> These are the gardens of the Desert, these
> The unshorn fields, boundless and beautiful,
> For which the speech of England has no name—
> The Prairies.

Then follows almost a catalogue of the stock elements of prairie description: the undulating grass, the flowers, the comparison with the sea, the "island groves," and the distant forest line.

In the second long paragraph, Bryant turns his mind from the present scene to the past and imagines a history for the prairie. Accepting the same belief that Flower did, that the Indian mounds were actually built by a pre-Indian people, "a race that long has passed away," he imagines that they were building the mounds

> while yet the Greek
> Was hewing the Pentelicus to forms
> Of symmetry, and rearing on its rock
> The glittering Parthenon.

The gentle, pastoral "mound-builders," he imagines, were slaughtered by Indians, "roaming hunter tribes, warlike and fierce," and he concludes this section with a melodramatic fantasy in which a fugitive mound-builder joins his Indian conquerors:

> he chose
> A bride among their maidens, and at length

> Seemed to forget—yet ne'er forgot—the wife
> Of his first love, and her sweet little ones,
> Butchered, amid their shrieks, with all his race.

The third paragraph is a meditation on historical change. The Indians who displaced the "mound-builders" have now themselves gone west, and "nearer to the Rocky Mountains, sought / A wilder hunting-ground." The beaver and bison, too, have left the prairies. Such changes are attributed to divine will:

> Thus change the forms of being. Thus arise
> Races of living things, glorious in strength,
> And perish, as the quickening breath of God
> Fills them, or is withdrawn.

The fourth verse-paragraph brings the poem full circle, as Bryant returns to the present. Despite the departure of the beaver and the bison, the prairie is full of living things: insects, birds, snakes, deer, and bees. The hum of the bee suggests the settlers soon to come to the prairies:

> I listen long
> To his domestic hum, and think I hear
> The sound of that advancing multitude
> Which soon shall fill these deserts. From the ground
> Comes up the laugh of children, the soft voice
> Of maidens, and the sweet and solemn hymn
> Of Sabbath worshippers. The low of herds
> Blends with the rustling of the heavy grain
> Over the dark brown furrows. All at once
> A fresher wind sweeps by, and breaks my dream,
> And I am in the wilderness alone.

Bryant brought to the Illinois prairie a fully articulated ideology of the American landscape that makes "The Prairies" quite different from the impressions of the English travelers, whose frames of reference, for both nature and society, are European. For Bryant, as for his close friend the painter Thomas Cole, the American landscape offered an sublimity potentially morally and spiritually superior to European natural sublimity. European painters and poets looked for ruins and other such reminders of humanity in their landscapes to humanize the scene and place the scenes within a context of human time. Bryant and Cole found in the very emptiness of the American wilderness a higher spirituality, since no sign of human beings intruded between the viewer and the embodiment of God in nature. This is the idea expressed, for example, in Bryant's much quoted sonnet "To Cole, the Painter, Departing for Europe" (1829), in which Bryant describes first the American landscape and then European ones, which show "everywhere the trace of men," and admonishes Cole to "keep that earlier, wilder image bright" (116).[5]

Bryant also shared with Cole a tendency to see in landscapes intimations of what has been called the Course of Empire theme, after Cole's 1836 sequence of paintings depicting the rise and decline of a civilization. Bryant devoted many poems to a cyclic theory of history in which civilizations, almost like plants, undergo a process of birth, flowering, and decay. Often these civilizations are Indian tribes. In "A Walk at Sunset," for example, the speaker lets his mind wander as he surveys a wooded landscape and imagines a time before the Indians came, then the period of the rule of the "hunter tribes," and finally the present when the speaker, "the offspring of another race," stands on the site and teaches "the quiet shades the strains of this new tongue" (28). The meanings Bryant attaches to the Course of Empire theme are ambiguous. It sometimes seems cautionary, a warning to his own country against deterioration of moral purpose. At other times, it seems fatalistic, suggesting that civilizations decline inevitably, regardless of their conduct.[6]

In "The Prairies," Bryant attempts to read the Illinois prairie in terms of both themes: the American sublime and the Course of Empire. An attempt, literally, to make something out of nothing, the poem begins and ends with the speaker alone in the great, empty, "encircling vastness." In the course of the poem, he attempts to fill the emptiness with meaning—the presence of God in the landscape, an imagined history correlated with European history, a vision of a civilization to come. But the effort to read this landscape in the same way that he had read more familiar Eastern landscapes becomes increasingly strained, and at the end, almost as if swept away by the

---

5. For good treatments of the "American sublime" in Bryant and Cole, see Donald A. Ringe, "Kindred Spirits: Bryant and Cole," and Charles L. Sanford, "The Concept of the Sublime in the Works of Thomas Cole and William Cullen Bryant."

6. Bryant's attitude toward western settlement is well treated in David J. Baxter, "The Dilemma of Progress: Bryant's Continental Vision," and Paul A. Newlin, "*The Prairie* and 'The Prairies': Cooper's and Bryant's Views of Manifest Destiny."

"fresher wind," his elaborate visionary structure collapses, and he is left at the point at which he began: "in the wilderness alone."

The opening description of the prairie landscape is governed by Bryant's expectations for the American sublime, untouched by any relic of humanity's presence. The prairie is empty; that is its great virtue. Here the observer directly encounters the handiwork of God, unmediated by human beings' less perfect work:

> Man hath no part in all this glorious work;
> The hand that built the firmament hath heaved
> And smoothed these verdant swells, and sown their slopes
> With herbage, planted them with island groves,
> And hedged them round with forests.

The landscape under its arching sky thus becomes a temple, the prairie a "fitting floor" and the sky a "vault" for "this magnificent temple of the sky."

Of course, one human being is in the landscape: the speaker. The unnamed, timeless innocence of nature can be only a hypothetical construct that necessarily must collapse for the poem to begin at all—as a verbal, cultural construct. Bryant's observer rides into the scene and colonizes it with a name and a gaze: "dilated sight" that "takes in the encircling vastness." The myth of an American sublime with no touch of the human can be only a myth as long as there is a human observer to report it.

The Course of Empire theme introduced in the second verse-paragraph is similarly problematical. Bryant is scrupulously consistent in including no mark of human beings in the landscape to suggest his imaginary history of the mound-builders; only the sound of his horse's hooves turns his thoughts to "the dead of other days." This is enough to inspire an elaborate, though imaginary, "history" for the prairies, a narrative of rising and falling civilizations correlated with European history. While "the Greek" was building the Pentelicus and the Parthenon, the gentle, agricultural "mound-builders" were cultivating their fields. They are violently displaced by "the red man," a nomadic race whose culture is built on war and hunting. Now the Indians have moved west and are being displaced by another stable, agricultural culture: that of the white settlers.

In this middle section of the poem, the point of view shifts from the initial organizing, colonizing gaze to a long, visionary perspective that summons up scenes from a fantasy history within which the immediate landscape is placed. The most obvious function of this historical fantasizing is to provide a Romantic frisson, to place the otherwise innocuous scene within a context of gothic melodrama. The meaning of the fantasy is less obvious. The first problem is a basic contradiction between the theme of the natural sublime and that of the Course of Empire. Are the prairies a holy place in which "man hath no part," or do they have a long and violent human history? Bryant experiments with both interpretations but leaves the contradiction unresolved.

Bryant's fantasy-history is also divided between two attitudes toward the past: a Romantic fatalism and a moralistic reading. On the one hand, civilizations rise and fall inevitably, as "the quickening breath of God / Fills them, or is withdrawn." On the other hand, all civilizations are not equal in Bryant's eyes, and a divine justice is at work in the displacement of the "warlike and fierce" Indians by white, agricultural settlers very much like the gentle mound-builders.

The interpretations of the Illinois prairie in "The Prairies" are not entirely consistent expressions of ideologies of western settlement. Bryant tended to present the themes of the American sublime and the Course of Empire in aesthetic or moralistic terms (and many of his critics have followed him in this). But these ideas perform cultural work as well; both serve to suppress troubling questions of western settlement and make white imperialism appear innocent or even divinely ordained. In his "sublime" representation of the prairie, Bryant draws on the familiar convention that the prairies were completely empty when white settlers arrived. The notion that the prairies were a "desert," an unpeopled Eden outside time, was of course false. As John Mack Faragher has recently brilliantly shown, in *Sugar Creek: Life on the Illinois Prairie,* the white settlers in Illinois encountered a stable, well-developed Indian culture, in many ways oddly like their own, which they displaced by force of arms. The assertion, familiar in the discourse of later commemorations of the frontier experience as well as in Bryant, that the field of settlement was a "howling wilderness" or an empty "desert" was self-serving. If the frontier were empty, whether as a virgin Eden or a howling wilderness, the whole question of the ethics of displacing an indigenous population could be suppressed.

Bryant's alternative notion that the prairies were not innocent of human history but were the recently vacated site of the rise and fall of empires to which the white race was a natural heir filled similar cultural needs. In Bryant's fantasy-history, the nonexistent mound-builders are linked with white civilization so thoroughly that the white settlers seem their natural heirs and the Indian control of the land only a temporary aberration. The mound-builders are represented as a peaceful, agricultural people with a highly developed culture, as opposed to the nomadic, primitive, bloodthirsty Indians who usurped their land, and they are provided with an imaginary history that parallels white European history, the mounds being built at the same time the Greeks were building the Parthenon. By displacement, white settlement is represented as a peaceful entry into an unoccupied land, while the violence that accompanied it is transferred back upon the Indians' treatment of the mound-builders, so that the Indians, rather than the whites, appear to be the violent usurpers and the destroyers of peace, order, and culture.

Bryant's treatment of the themes of the American sublime and the Course of Empire, then, are ideological formations justifying imperialist expansion, but "The Prairies" also implies broader and less ideological meditations on the meaning of American nature and the implications of settlement. The poem explores a paradox implicit in much previous prairie description as well as in other nature writing of the period: the paradox of exalting the sublimity of unmediated nature while at the same time calling for that sublimity to be destroyed through settlement. This paradox perhaps expressed a deeper cultural anxiety about the prospects of America. Timeless nature is being summoned into history, and an empire is being planted in the sublime landscape. Can this empire escape the fate of Greece and Rome—and the mound-builders? Can it transcend the cycles of history in which "races of living things" arise and perish, as "the quickening breath of God / Fills them, or is withdrawn"?

The prairies are empty at the beginning of the poem. By the end, Bryant has filled them, not only with the birds and bees that make "the great solitude" "quick with life," but with an imagined past and an anticipated future. At the beginning, "man hath no part in all this glorious work," but by the end, the prairies have been thoroughly humanized, assimilated to human history and culture. The poetic responsibility for what amounts to an act of desecration of the prairies' "magnificent temple of the sky" anticipates the responsibility to be borne by that "advancing multitude" soon to populate the prairies. How that responsibility will be carried out is a question Bryant leaves open as the poem ends.

Perhaps the principal interest of "The Prairies" lies in its attempts to interpret the prairie within frameworks formed for other, less uncompromising landscapes and the failure of each attempt. Confronted by the immense blankness of the prairie, Bryant tries first to contain it within his myth of the unmediated sublime, as a natural temple. As if sensing the inadequacy of this reading, he turns to the only partially compatible one of the prairie as the historic site of the violent course of empire, a reading that ends in stagy melodrama. He finally moves to a reading of the prairie as the waiting cradle of a future civilization, peopling the prairie in his imagination with "transplanted Elizabethan milkmaids, elfin children and God-loving happy rustics," as Paul A. Newlin calls them (37). Bryant has tried to fill the emptiness of the prairie with three elaborate interpretive structures. None is adequate, and appropriately "a fresher wind" sweeps them away. Bryant is left, as he was at the beginning, "in the wilderness alone."

Prairie Narratives

The brief, tentative accounts of the prairie in travelers' narratives are elaborated into extensive explorations of the meaning of the prairie in three important Illinois books: Eliza Farnham's *Life in Prairie Land,* John Regan's *Emigrant's Guide to the Western States of America,* and Francis Grierson's *Valley of Shadows.* Farnham's and Regan's books were written in the closing years of the frontier period in Illinois (1846 and 1848?); Grierson's was written long afterward (1909) but reflects the author's memories of an Illinois childhood in the 1850s. The prairie, much more than an incidental setting, is a living presence in all three of these books; the central action in each is an encounter with the prairie and an attempt to understand it in terms of human life, to give it a cultural meaning.

The basic materials of *Life in Prairie Land, The Emigrant's Guide,* and *The Valley of Shadows,* despite the radical differences among the books, have much in common. All three report temporary residences on the Illinois prairie. Farnham came to Illinois from the East in 1835 and went back to the East in 1839. Regan emigrated from

Scotland in 1842 and returned there in 1847. (He later returned permanently to Illinois, but his book deals only with his first residence.) Grierson as a child accompanied his parents to Illinois in 1849 and left with them in 1858. All three books are thus based on simple patterns of arrival and departure.

The experiences of the three on the Illinois prairie were very different, however, and the differences are reflected in the various genres in which the three writers cast their stories. To oversimplify, *Life in Prairie Land* is a spiritual autobiography, *The Emigrant's Guide* a comic novel, and *The Valley of Shadows* a symbolist narrative. Significantly, the fit between the experience and the genre in which it is narrated is imperfect in all three books. *Life in Prairie Land* has been classified as travel writing, autobiography, and fiction, *The Emigrant's Guide* as a settler's handbook, autobiography, and comic sketches, and *The Valley of Shadows* as fiction and autobiography. The authors themselves are self-conscious about the genres in which they are working. Regan gives his book a utilitarian title, *The Emigrant's Guide,* and a novelistic subtitle, *Backwoods and Prairies.* Grierson insists in his preface that his book is "not a novel, but the recollections of scenes and episodes of my early life in Illinois and Missouri" (vii), thereby acknowledging the ambiguity of its genre. It is as though traditional genres are felt to be inadequate for prairie experience; something is left over and unaccounted for. These books thus seem interestingly unfinished; the question of what discursive form can convey frontier experience has been raised but not fully answered.

Life in Prairie Land

Life in Prairie Land is so little known, despite at least two modern editions and some recent attention by feminist critics, that a brief summary may be helpful. The book opens in St. Louis, with Farnham and her brother Hal on their way to visit their sister Mary and her husband, who are living on the prairie up the Illinois River.[7] After a long steamboat journey, they arrive at "Prairie

---

7. John Hallwas (1981–82) has supplied the names of people and places, which Farnham for the most part suppresses. Mary's husband, for example, was named John M. Roberts, and their farm was near Groveland in Tazewell County. Since my reading attaches some significance to these suppressions, I confine myself in this summary to information actually given in the book.

Lodge," Mary's home, and spend several weeks there. Farnham then moves into lodgings in a wretchedly filthy "Sucker" (Illinois) house, while waiting for a new house to be finished, into which she will move with her new husband, who is abruptly and unexpectedly introduced and identified only as "Mr. F——." The new house is rented to someone else, so they move into a two-room cottage in an unidentified small town and set up housekeeping. Farnham has a baby and moves back to Prairie Lodge, where Mary is dying of tuberculosis. Mary's death is followed by the death of Farnham's baby, in the midst of a prairie drought accompanied by a malaria epidemic. Farnham reports her partial recovery from "black despair," and Part 1 of the book ends: "Thus with heaviest afflictions on the one hand, and cheering hopes on the other, closed the second year of Life in the Prairie Land" (168).

Part 2 is sharply different from Part 1, abandoning the more or less continuous narrative in favor of a series of descriptive chapters on prairie life and an account of several journeys through Illinois, first to Dixon and the Rock River country, then down through Springfield to Alton, climaxing with a long description of an idyllic excursion with some friends for a picnic on a bluff overlooking the Mississippi River. The book ends with the return of Farnham's husband from an unexplained journey and their departure from Illinois for the East.

Even this bare summary suggests one feature of the structure of *Life in Prairie Land*. The two parts of the book present a pattern of crisis and recovery in the heart of the natural world, a pattern strongly reminiscent of Wordsworth's *The Prelude*, to which Farnham is clearly indebted. Part 1 leads Farnham to a spiritual crisis from which she begins a recovery as the first part ends; Part 2 is devoted to the completion of the process. The entire book thus rocks on that central sentence, between the "heaviest afflictions" of Part 1 and the "cheering hopes" of Part 2.

Farnham describes her crisis in religious language, though her conclusions are not orthodox. Traumatized by the death of her sister and her child, she succumbs to despair. A local pastor gives her a copy of the Psalms, and as she reads them "the cloud began to pass away" (167). The comfort she finds is secular and rationalist, however, and very different from Mary's quiet religious faith. "The comfort which I found," she writes, "was no miraculous shining forth of anything external to myself; it was no overflowing fountain which poured itself out, independent of my own state of mind, such as many seem to have found, but simply a more exalted action of some powers which I had always possessed, and a partial subduing of others" (168).

Most readers of *Life in Prairie Land* seem to have sensed in the book a transformation of Farnham much more general and fundamental than this recovery from debilitating grief, a transformation hinted at, perhaps, in her rather elliptical reference to the "exalted action" of some of her powers and the "partial subduing" of others. In her treatment of *Life in Prairie Land,* the feminist critic Annette Kolodny has emphasized the theme of self-discovery. Noting that Farnham in her preface says that the West "presents itself to my mind in the light of a strong and generous parent" (xxiii) and that she tends to use familial imagery, as when she imagines trees to be "elder brothers" (46), Kolodny concludes that Farnham "found in Illinois a natural world that, imaginatively at least, seemed to compensate for the family she had lost in childhood" (109). Kolodny's view of the book as a maturation narrative is certainly correct, but her emphasis on regression, compensation, and reparation as the components of that maturation should be reviewed and perhaps qualified. Farnham's experience in Illinois is not so much a passive return to the security of a fantasized primary family as an active construction of the prairie as a microcosmic field of struggle and the discovery within herself of "some powers which [she] had always possessed" that she could bring to that struggle.

Life in Prairie Land is an oddly constructed book, full of unexpected ellipses on the one hand and almost gratuitous episodic amplifications on the other. We are well into the book before we learn that Farnham's traveling companion is her brother; her brother-in-law remains a silent, nameless figure throughout her extended stay at Prairie Lodge; and her engagement and marriage to "Mr. F——" are passed over in silence. In the second part of the book, Mr. F—— disappears as mysteriously as he appeared and is absent for sixteen months; only upon his return are we told that he has been in California and are given the unexplained information that "it had been in his power to save the lives, and restore the liberties of several of his countrymen" (259). The suppression of almost all the names of what are obviously real places has a similarly disorienting effect, as if we were being deliberately deprived of landmarks.

While basic information about settings, characters, and motivations is withheld, the narrative is amplified at several points with inset narratives only loosely attached to the main action. The first of these is "the story of the dark man" told by Mary in Chapter 10, the story of a neighbor who lost his young wife and child to malaria and now lives at Prairie Lodge, "sick, dejected, melancholy" (853–54). Similar inset narratives are the story of a prairie fire in the second part and an extended story (252–59) of a farm wife, whose husband did not return from a hunting trip and was found drowned the following spring. The effect of these narrative strategies is a narrative constantly folding back upon itself, embedding miniature versions of itself within its larger structure.

By far the most important of these embedded narratives is the prolonged account of the death of Mary and of Farnham's final conversations with her, which stretches out over the last five chapters of Part 1. The length and central placement of this episode suggest its centrality to the book's meaning. Most of this section is given over to long monologues by Mary, in which she recounts the story of her sister's and her childhood and her later life on the prairie, thus opening a window into the past and giving the emotional roots of the present action. The parallels between Mary and her sister are so close that Mary becomes a double for Farnham, enacting emotional issues in a distanced, displaced form.

Briefly, Mary recalls an early childhood spent with her sister in close communion with nature. Their mother died when they were both young children. "From that day," Mary says, "we had no longer a home in common; when we met, it was as visitors" (148). The sisters were separated and sent to live with relatives far apart; they did not see each other for seven years. Those seven years, from nine to sixteen for Mary, taught her "to shrink continually from the world, to regard it as an enemy ever on the watch to destroy my peace, ever waiting with lies and deceit, to lead me away from my true path" (148). Farnham herself, by Mary's testimony, spent the crucial seven years under "the tyranny of a selfish, passionate woman, and that woman . . . an Atheist—a defier of her God!" (150). Reunited briefly, Farnham shocked Mary by her skepticism and her dismissal of religion as "delusive mummery" (150). Separated again after a few weeks, Mary married and moved to Illinois, while Eliza went "to seek the education and mental culture which should have been the work of earlier years" (151).

The rest of Mary's narrative concerns her journey into Illinois with her new husband to build a home. The journey becomes in the telling a spiritual quest for Mary, in which she gains not only a home but a way of regarding the world as something other than an enemy. She is reborn on the prairie:

> At last we emerged upon the great prairie which extends from the Wabash, west and north, nearly three hundred miles. Here the magnificence of the country to which we were bound began to appear. I remember, as we journeyed day after day across its heaving, verdant bosom, that I seemed to be living in a new world. All the noise, all the selfish hurry and turmoil in which my past years had been spent, faded away. They seemed as remote as if the barrier of eternity had been placed between me and them. A new creation was around me. (151)

In telling the story of her life on the prairie, Mary does not soften the hardships; she tells of prolonged illnesses, the destruction of the crops by a prairie fire, and other trials. But she never wavers in her strength and joy in her new life.

Mary's narrative of rebirth on a maternal prairie, a "heaving, verdant bosom," told as she lies dying, encapsulates Farnham's own story as it unfolds throughout the book: the journey into the prairie, the encounters both with sublime beauty and with hardship and degradation, the initiation into sexuality and marriage, and, most important, the sense of the natural world as "an enemy ever on the watch to destroy my peace," a perception of the world from which the prairie has delivered Mary. Mary dies hoping that her sister will come to take the same comfort from religion that she has taken. Farnham, in the despair that follows her sister's and son's deaths, tries to follow Mary's example but cannot. She finds comfort, but it is not supernatural: "I found no power superior to my own mind, pulling down the one and setting up the other—it depended on myself" (168). Mary's other lesson, however—of learning to be at home in the world—is one that Farnham gradually learns. These are the "cheering hopes" with which the first part of *Life in Prairie Land* ends.

Farnham's conflicts and her triumph over them are inscribed in her representation of the prairie. Her account of her First View of the Prairie, for example, closely parallels the one she assigns to Mary in language and effect:

I can never forget the thrill which this first unbounded view on a prairie gave me. I afterwards saw many more magnificent—many richer in all elements of beauty, many so extensive that this appeared a mere meadow beside them, but no other had the charm of this. I have looked upon it a thousand times since, and wished in my selfishness that it might remain unchanged; that neither buildings, fences, trees, nor living things should change its features while I live, that I might carry this first portrait of it unchanged to my grave. I see it now, its soft outline swelling against the clear eastern sky, its heaving surface pencilled with black and brown lines, its borders fringed with the naked trees! (26–27)

Behind this "picturesque" account (a "portrait . . . pencilled with black and brown lines"), we can sense some of the maternal qualities that appear in Mary's description. The prairie's "soft outline" heaves here as the prairie "bosom" did in Mary's description. But if the prairie here suggests the security and joy of maternal nurturing, the account is also heavily nostalgic and shot through with fears of loss. Farnham places this first view of an idyllic, untouched prairie far in the past even as she describes it, prefacing her description with prairies she would see "afterwards." Even as she describes the scene, she anticipates its loss as civilization encroaches on it.

What complicates Farnham's presentation of the prairie as a "generous parent" offering security at a maternal bosom is a countertheme running through the book, which presents the prairie as a dangerous, sinister force that, without warning, can destroy anything human encroaching on it. The beautiful, verdant, and hospitable prairie of which Mary's home, Prairie Lodge, seems an organic part can, with a few weeks' drought, turn into a pestilential wasteland, breeding contagion that snatches away both Farnham's sister and her baby.

For the most part, though, the negative inscription of the prairie does not appear in the main action but is banished to the embedded stories, all tales of destruction and loss. It is as if Farnham's presentation of the world as "an enemy ever on the watch to destroy my peace," excluded from the main narrative, rises in the inset stories like the return of the repressed. The story of the dark man in Part 1, which anticipates the deaths of Mary and Farnham's baby, is of this sort, as is the story of the drowned man in Part 2. The most extended presentation of the prairie as treacherous and fatal, however, is the prairie fire episode in Part 2 (175–85). Here a family settles in an idyllic, gardenlike part of the prairie near two groves of trees. While the husband and son are away buying supplies, the pregnant wife and small children remain alone. A prairie fire sweeps down upon them, and they barely escape by fleeing to a plowed field. The house and all their supplies are destroyed. The mother tries to feed her children on groundnuts until an icy storm comes after the fire. She gives birth to a stillborn baby, and she and the children are all dying when the husband and older son return. The husband curses the day "when he trusted the treacherous beauty that invited him there," and the scene ends with a reiteration of the same dangerous ambiguity in the prairie landscape: "The plain below is still unchanged. It is the same rich, green expanse in summer; the same bleak, howling waste in winter" (184).

Farnham presents this story as a true incident, and there is no reason to believe that it is not. Her treatment of it is very personal, however. Her characterization of the prairie as "treacherous beauty" that can lure a victim into its "rich, green expanse" and suddenly destroy her, amounting almost to personification, restates the emotional issue of seeing the world as "an enemy ever on the watch to destroy my peace."

The comfortable cabin, suddenly destroyed, and the icy plowed field, where the wife and children in the prairie fire episode perish, are only two of many indoor and outdoor spaces that express Farnham's spiritual progress toward being at home in the world. Farnham moves from room to room, from the miserable cabin on board the steamboat to her temporary lodging at Prairie Lodge and the grim, filthy Sucker cabin to her two-room cottage with Mr. F——, describing in sometimes wearisome detail her feats of housecleaning. Her treatment of homes emphasizes alienation from nature and integration with it. Mary's Prairie Lodge, with its neatness and order, surrounded by roses brought from the East and representing a continuity of family and home, is the chief contrast to the filthy cabins that usually represent civilization in Prairie Land. Here the indoors is not contrasted with the beautiful outdoors but is integrated with it, a nest in the prairie. In the debased Sucker cabin, however, human meanness and ugliness intrude on natural beauty. Farnham surveys the filth of the cabin and walks outdoors: "Nature was pure and beautiful here as elsewhere. The deep wood, with its clear leafy aisles, was doubly inviting, by contrast, with the filth from which I had just escaped" (75). The emblem that presides over this strain of the book might be the image of Farnham, well-scrubbed and neatly dressed in her eastern clothes, sitting on her bed in the few square feet of floor space she has scoured and walled off with hanging quilts from the chaos and filth of the Sucker cabin (76ff.). The point is not just housekeeping but the tendency, through fear, "to shrink continually from the world."

The quest, through the many rooms of *Life in Prairie Land*, for a mature sense of being at home in the world culminates in an idyllic episode at the end of the book, in which Farnham and a group of friends make an excursion to the bluffs overlooking the Mississippi River near Alton. Farnham and a friend precede the rest of the rather large party as a "committee of selection" to pick a location for the picnic. They ascend the bluff and at the top find their ideal place:

> On the very pinnacle of the bluff, the east side of which was thickly wooded and the west opening upon the river, we found a little shaded nook, just large enough to admit our number. Here, after the vines and light undergrowth had been cleared away, we spread out white napkins, table cloths, &c., and laid out our simple refreshments. Two or three loaves of bread, a bottle of cream, some golden butter, a trio of cold chickens, and a loaf of plain family cake of the largest size, constituted the whole. (248)

Here is the last of the many living spaces that follow each other in the book, and significantly it combines indoors and outdoors, an enclosed "nook" barely large enough to contain the party and yet set in the vast spaces of nature.

Farnham and her friends spend the day singing, talking, and exploring the area overlooking the river. The prairie pastoral ends with this description of Farnham's and her companions' mood:

> We had little relish for our second meal. The sense of mere existence had been such a joy and blessing all the day, that the common pleasures of life had lost their power to engage our faculties. We were merry, but our merriment was not that which flashes in fitful gleams from the troubled heart, or breaks forth for a moment to subside on the recurrence of care into a deeper gravity than before. It was founded on the deep, full, inward joy which we had been all the day drawing from the pure and beautiful world around us. (250)

A "deep, full, inward joy": the words echo the dying Mary's, when she describes the "unalloyed pleasure" (157) she learned to take from prairie land, and contrast sharply with the emotions of the embattled Farnham at the beginning of the book, who feels the world to be an enemy.

Life in Prairie Land is a curious book, on the one hand, a Romantic travel narrative looking outward at the world and, on the other, an inward-looking exploration of spiritual crisis and recovery. Yet the two strains in the book do not conflict with one another but produce a strangely touching account of an Illinois landscape charged with emotional meaning. The beautiful and the sublime of Farnham's prairie take on the colorings of maternal ambivalence: the "heaving, verdant bosom" of nurturing, along with the "treacherous beauty" that can destroy or withdraw forever. Farnham's victory in the book is in confronting this ambivalence and moving beyond it to a sense of being at home in the world.

The Emigrant's Guide to the Western States of America

The lost first edition of John Regan's *Emigrant's Guide to the Western States of America* appeared within two or three years after the publication of *Life in Prairie Land*. It, too, tells the story of a few years residence on the Illinois prairie and draws on the conventions of prairie description in a highly personal way. There the comparison stops. Farnham contemplates the blank page of the prairie and inscribes on it an ambivalently maternal nature and her own spiritual struggle with that internalized nature. Regan makes the Illinois prairie an imaginative space for the inscription of social comedy. His basic social unit is not the privatized nuclear family but the village and the neighborhood, and his Illinois is the setting of a comic but searching inquiry into the new forms of social organization evolving on the prairie.

Regan was a Scottish schoolmaster who went to Illinois in 1842, when he was twenty-three years old, with his new bride, Elizabeth. They bought a forty-acre homestead in the village of Virgil in the Spoon River area, where Regan farmed and taught in the village school for three years. They apparently moved to Knoxville in 1845 and lived there for two years before returning temporarily to Scotland in 1847. Regan took another teaching job in the village of Whitletts in Ayrshire and wrote *The Emigrant's Guide,* a first edition of which seems to have been published sometime between 1848 and 1850, though no copies have been located. The second edition in 1852 contains a number of references to the first edition and incorporates several letters written in response to it. A third edition, retitled *The Western Wilds of America,* appeared in 1859. Regan and his wife, who by then had three children, returned to Illinois in 1852 or 1853, where he taught school again and opened a book bindery in Knoxville. He later edited a series of newspapers, including the *Knoxville Journal,* the *Elmwood Observer,* the *Elmwood Messenger,* and the *Maquon Times.* He died in 1893.[8]

There are two books buried in *The Emigrant's Guide.* Of the book's forty chapters, about ten are indeed an emigrant's guide, giving information about routes to the West, prices of land, and methods of farming. Regan gives instructions for building a log cabin, making sun-dried bricks, and even cooking a frontier meal. The other thirty chapters are a lively comic narrative about Regan's adventures in Illinois, told with all the resources of fiction: vividly realized characters, artfully plotted incidents, and rich, comic dialogue. Even the book's double title seems to point to its split nature, *The Emigrant's Guide* for the informational chapters, *Backwoods and Prairies* for the fictional ones.

Regan is a highly self-conscious writer, and he makes comic capital even out of the split between didacticism and fiction in his book. At one point, he apologizes for a discursive section on the difficulties of emigration and promises "another Backwoods story" when it is over (112). At another point, he concludes a set of instructions about how to build a log cabin by saying that "this sort of dry description . . . will not do" (309) and launches into a broadly comic tale called "Tom Randall's Raising Bee," into which he inserts another comic story by the humorist Dan Marble.

If the theme of the emigrant's-guide chapters is how to succeed economically on the frontier, the theme of the backwoods-and-prairies stories is social relationships, the kind of democratic society evolving on the western prairie. Regan is concerned about providing practical information for prospective emigrants, but he is even more interested in exploring "Western manners" and the opportunity they offer for a satisfactory life. "There is all the difference in the world," he writes, "between the American seaboard and the interior, in the manners of the people. On the coast, the manners of older

---

8. John Hallwas has done the basic research on Regan's life. See Hallwas (1984), from which my account is taken.

countries in some measure prevail, and a just estimate of the true character of the people cannot be formed from that source. From the firm woof, not the ravelled edge, of American society, I have culled my pictures of Western manners, and they are taken from the life" (iii–iv). Significantly, he finds the best form for his "pictures of Western manners" to be a warm, sympathetic comedy.

Regan is a born storyteller. "I find that the best way of conveying information is by telling a story," he writes (204). The role he chooses for himself in his book is that of observer, recorder, and narrator. At one point, a neighbor asks him, "Now, aint you the man I've seen at some of our meetin's lately, writing away like sixty?" (160). At another point, he quotes his favorite poet, Robert Burns: "A chiel's among ye takin' notes, / An' faith he'll prent it" (273). Active and involved in the practical affairs of the community as Regan is, he is also "a chiel among ye takin' notes" and processing his experiences and observations into narrative. *The Emigrant's Guide* is not so much a collection of comic stories as a continuous account of the production of comic narrative, as frontier experience is shaped to the mode of comedy.

The prairie is a continuous presence in *The Emigrant's Guide*, as it is in *Life in Prairie Land*. Regan is closely attentive to the landscape. Here, for example, is his First View of the Prairie:

> By and bye the forest began to thin, and we emerged upon the "Prairie." We ascended a rising ground to the right, to take a survey of this celebrated feature of the western landscape. Before us, far far to the east, lay one vast plain of verdure and flowers, without house or home, or anything to break in upon the uniformity of the scene, except the shadow of a passing cloud. To the right and left long points of timber, like capes and headlands, stretched in the blue distance—the light breezes of the morning brushing along the young grass and blue and pink flowers—the strong sun-light pouring down every where—and the singular silence which pervaded the scene—produced a striking effect upon the mind. My feelings, indeed, were of the most elated and enraptured description. I had heard of Eden and Elysium. Was it possible that their beauties could surpass these? (42)

There are many other such celebrations of the prairie in the course of Regan's many comings and goings in the book.

But Regan's prairie is very different from Farnham's, despite the closeness in time of their Illinois experiences. Farnham's book looks backward historically as well as personally, in spite of recounting her visits to villages and towns, to a time when the prairie was almost empty, with isolated houses scattered miles apart. His rather conventional reference to "Eden" and "Elysium" notwithstanding, Regan does not look back to some original personal relationship with nature but forward to the growth of rural communities and neighborhoods. His basic figure is not the lonely, Bryant-like figure on horseback contemplating the prairie but the busy villager going about his daily routine within a social network of neighbors.

Regan's comic "pictures of Western manners" include visits with settlers, a trial in a frontier court, a "protracted meeting," a camp meeting, an Independence Day celebration, and other picturesque incidents. One especially successful story is entitled "Driving a Trade" and is offered as an illustration of the fact that cash is scarce on the frontier and complex systems of barter spring up as an alternative to cash transactions.[9] "Driving a Trade" goes far beyond this simple purpose though; twelve pages long, it is a fully realized comic short story. Regan wants to buy a horse, which will cost about fifty dollars, but he has no cash. He does have "credit" for sixty-eight dollars with seven creditors who have unpaid school fees, so he launches out to "drive a trade." He rides a mare borrowed from his good friend Bill Hendryx over to the farm of "Squire" Philip Ailsworth, who will trade him a fifty-dollar horse for a seventy-dollar wagon, giving him the difference in cash. The carpenter Charles Cain says he will build a wagon for sixty-eight dollars in trade and lists the things he needs:

> Let's see. Wal, I want a good cow badly, an' a thousand shingles, an' half-a-dozen sheep, an' some, an' some winder glass, an'—an'—an' some smith work, maybe two days, an' some teamin', three days, an' three days' ploughin', an' a ton of Timothy, an' some things at the store, sich as leather, nails, an' a whole *lot* of notions. An' see hyar—couldn't you scare me up a barrel o' flour, an' about a dozen o' pork barrels? If you can turn me out sich things as these, I don't know but we may make a trade on't yet. (208)

Regan agrees and rides on, contemplating the carpenter's "multitudinous wants." In the course of the day, he visits Jesse Fielding,

---

9. This is the section reprinted in Hallwas (1986:90–95).

an English immigrant with whom he trades for the pork barrels; a Yankee named Martin Luther Sly, who supplies the cow; a lazy, worthless neighbor named Portman Hoyt, who refuses to honor Regan's credit for teaching his children; and a thrifty, industrious neighbor named Righteous Mead, who pays his bill in cash. Regan's credit at the village store supplies the store goods, a man with a "shingle machine" furnishes the shingles, and a twelve-dollar loan from Bill Hendryx completes the negotiations. Regan has his horse.

"Driving a Trade" presents in miniature Regan's methods in the entire book. Characteristically, he is in motion throughout the story, riding from neighbor to neighbor. Regan is a family man and a schoolteacher, but his wife is never named and seldom mentioned, there are no significant scenes of domestic life, and he never describes his work in the schoolroom (although there is one amusing scene in which the school board examines prospective teachers for certification [239–43]). The book is largely given over to Regan's travels, whether short local trips, such as his trading rounds, or extended journeys, such as the "seven days' tour of exploration of the prairies" reported in chapter 32. Regan's stories of his travels focus equally on the prairie landscape and the human institutions growing up on the prairie. As he rides from neighbor to neighbor in "Driving a Trade," he describes the countryside: "As I now wended my way along the bottom lands of Spoon river, the scenery was beyond description beautiful" (206). He gradually inscribes a network of human relationships on this landscape. The web of economic obligations that makes the horse trade possible is echoed in other episodes by other social relationships that bind the community together, whether through government, religion, law, or private friendship.

Regan's real subject in "Driving a Trade" is not the economics of barter but his neighbors. He remarks at the end of the story that the settlers say an immigrant never begins to thrive until he spends all his cash and has to start trading. The man with cash "remains ignorant of the real character of the people for a longer period than the man who goes out among them, sees them at home, and takes lessons beneath every roof. I can safely say I never learnt so much in one day before" (215).

Regan is remarkably clear-sighted about "Western manners," despite his frank advocacy of emigration. The freedom and opportunity of life on the open prairie has its dark side too, and Regan is quick to observe and report it. Free, unrestrained frontier trading may facilitate the flow of goods and services and enable Regan to convert his intangible assets into a good horse, but it also may encourage greed, as the carpenter's absurdly extended list of needs suggests. "This is the *evil* of 'trading,'" Regan remarks, "and not the mere trouble of the business. A disposition to overreach is imperceptibly acquired, at which the emigrant must not be too much astonished at first, but live on in hopes that the course of time will remove or abate the evil as the country fills up" (208). Freedom and the weakness of restraining laws can also lead to abuses by such people as Portman Hoyt, who can refuse to pay a legitimate debt by telling Regan, "By gauly, you may take it to the Squire's if you've a mind to. I haint got a red cent's worth more than what the law allows me, an' now you can't help yourself: can you?" (214). As he comically presents the frontier lawsuit in chapter 16, he also draws melancholy conclusions about its meaning for frontier democracy. After the decision, he walks out into the "solemn grandeur" of the forest and reflects, "Amidst Arcadian scenes . . . here was man. Into this Lycaonian retreat he had brought with him all his gods, all his idols, all his passions: the passions which more properly belong to the headlong haste and fierce competitions of older and more corrupt states, were here also" (106–7).

Despite such reservations as these about frontier institutions, Regan is on the whole affirmative about the western democratic experiment. "In the Western States," he writes,

> where the old world manners and feelings of pride and vanity have not yet obtained much footing, the emigrant observes that the people are much on an equality. . . . Every man is in a certain degree independent. A maxim with the Western man is this—"I am just as good as the next feller, an' he's as good as me; so that's all about it." The high, artificial style of living, which is confessedly very hollow, is unknown. With abundance of the necessaries of life, the people have in fact no "lower orders" to look down upon—no beggars, no paupers, no whining crew to whet a false conceit upon. There the "swinish multitude" are *bona fide* porkers, destined for the pickling tub at Christmas. (218)

The Emigrant's Guide culminates, as *Life in Prairie Land* does, with an outdoor excursion: a fishing trip to Lake Peoria that Regan takes with five of his Virgil friends. This extended episode (373–93) pulls together, as Farnham's Alton picnic does, the various strains of the book into one dynamic image. There are crucial differences, however. Farnham's companions remain vague, shadowy, and nameless figures, and her experience of a "a deep, full, inward joy" is essentially a private encounter with nature. Regan's fishing trip is essentially a celebration of friendship, of democratic social relationships based on equality and mutual respect. The fishermen get their seine by, typically, "driving a trade." They set off for Lake Peoria in two wagons on a beautiful day in Indian summer. Bill Hendryx has an encounter with a skunk that provides a great deal of low humor. Regan and his friend Charley Williams have a bardic contest in which they match poetic improvisations on the theme of the moon. The earnest Charley produces a lofty effusion, while Regan slyly works the skunk into his moon poem. There is a clash with two unsavory slave catchers, in which the Virgil citizens emerge triumphant over the representatives of slavery. All Regan's social ideals are encapsulated in this Waltonesque comedy: respect for human worth, disregard of social class, the melding of different cultures, instinctive resistance to such institutions as slavery, and social relationships based on trust rather than authority.

John Hallwas has perceptively written that the theme of *The Emigrant's Guide* is "the Americanization of John Regan" (1986:90). Shirreff, Dickens, Bryant, and even Farnham were visitors to the prairie; Regan was an immigrant, resolved to make a permanent home in prairie land. His prairie is not the product of the projective gaze of the First View but is gradually built up from a viewpoint within frontier society. The great emptiness on which Bryant projected his preconceptions is networked in *The Emigrant's Guide* by paths and wagon tracks; it has become the setting for a democratic society for which its open spaces, its natural grace, and its latent fecundity are potent symbols.

The Valley of Shadows

If the Illinois prairie is the field of personal spiritual development in *Life in Prairie Land* and of new social relationships in *The Emigrant's Guide,* it is a landscape vibrating with mystical meaning in Francis Grierson's *Valley of Shadows.* After a long career as a spiritualist, an eccentric improvisationalist on the piano in the salons of

the European nobility, and the author of several volumes of frag-
ile, idealistic essays, Grierson, at the age of sixty-one, turned his
mind back half a century and wrote his "Recollections of the Lincoln
Country, 1858–1863" (his original subtitle) in London.

The Valley of Shadows holds a curious place in American literary history, recurringly knocking for admission on the door of the
established canon and yet never quite admitted. The book was extravagantly praised when it appeared in 1909. Various reviewers
found it "poetic," "haunting," "uncanny," and "drenched in mysticism," and Shaemas O'Sheel, in the *New Republic,* praised it as
"unsurpassed by anything since Homer and Xenophon," as an evocation of war.[10] Yet the book had dropped out of sight by 1927,
the year of its author's death. O'Sheel tried to reawaken interest in
Grierson's works in 1931, with little success, and Roy P. Basler, in
The Lincoln Legend (1935), praised *The Valley of Shadows* as one of the
best literary treatments of Lincoln, again without much response.
Periodic critical rediscoveries of the book have prompted a series of
reissues and new editions. Theodore Spencer wrote a lengthy, ap-
preciative introduction to a new edition in 1948, to which Bernard
DeVoto contributed an even more glowing editor's note. Edmund
Wilson wrote a long, laudatory review of this edition in the *New
Yorker* and later included a substantial appreciation of the book in
Patriotic Gore (1962). Van Wyck Brooks, too, was an admirer of
Grierson's work and devoted considerable attention to it in *The Confident Years, 1885–1915* (1952) and *Scenes and Portraits* (1954). The
only book-length study of Grierson's work appeared in 1966 as a
volume in the Twayne United States Authors Series by Harold P.
Simonson, who also edited a new edition of *The Valley of Shadows*
in 1970. The most illuminating study of Grierson's major work appeared in 1982, in a section of Robert Bray's *Rediscoveries: Literature
and Place in Illinois*. Grierson has remained caviar to the general,
however; his name does not even appear, for example, in the recent
Columbia Literary History of the United States.

Explaining the paradox of a book's being extravagantly praised by
major critics over a period of eighty years and yet largely ignored by
most who read, study, and teach American literature must be dele-

---

10. Harold P. Simonson surveys the critical reception of *The Valley of Shadows* in
Francis Grierson (105–10), from which much of my account is taken.

gated to those who probe the mysteries of canon formation. One might hazard a guess, though, that one reason *The Valley of Shadows* has been so consistently marginalized in American studies is that it is something of a sport or a freak, hard to fit into any of the generally recognized traditions of American literature. Grierson does extremely well what nobody else even attempts: a symbolist interpretation of the American landscape, specifically the Illinois prairie in the 1850s. The result is a book of haunting power as well as undeniable oddity.

The first half of *The Valley of Shadows,* the Illinois portion (the second half consists of a series of loosely related sketches set farther west), re-creates, poetically and nostalgically, the prairie community of Grierson's childhood, a community full of signs and portents of the coming apocalypse of the Civil War. A fragmentary plot runs through this section of the book, involving the efforts of abolitionist settlers to smuggle escaped slaves along the Underground Railroad, against the efforts of proslavery neighbors. It culminates in a powerful camp-meeting scene that reaches a climactic ecstasy as a prairie storm breaks. The bodies of two young men killed during the meeting are brought to the platform. The son of the Southern sympathizer Minerva Wagner has been drowned in the river; the son of the abolitionist Kezia Jordan has been struck by lightning. The tableau, lit by flashes of lightning, of the mothers weeping over their Northern and Southern sons' bodies, before a field of mourners collapsed like "the dead and dying," while the exhorter cries that "Tophet is yawning," is an extraordinarily vivid portent of the holocaust about to envelop the nation (147–52).

Summary cannot suggest the quality of *The Valley of Shadows,* in which the slight action is set into a lush, vibrant evocation of the Illinois landscape. Grierson begins by recalling the prairie in his proem to the book:

> The early Jesuit missionaries often spoke of the Illinois prairie as a sea of grass and flowers. A breeze springs up from the shores of old Kentucky, or from across the Mississippi and the plains of Kansas, gathering force as the hours steal on, gradually changing the aspect of Nature by an undulating motion of the grass, until the breeze has become a gale, and behold the prairie a rolling sea! The pennant-like blades dip before the storm in low, rushing billows as of myriads of green birds skimming the surface. The grassy blades bend to the rhythm of Nature's music, and

when clouds begin to fleck the far horizon with dim, shifting vapours, shadows as of long grey wings swoop down over the prairie, while here and there immense fleeting veils rise and fall and sweep on towards the sky-line in a vague world of mystery and illusion. (2–3)

Grierson's prairie, while following the conventions initiated by the "early Jesuit missionaries," has undergone a transformation from a literal scene to "a vague world of mystery and illusion." These mysteries and illusions are explored throughout the book. Here, for example, is a representative passage, describing the morning glories that grow around the door of the log house in which the young Grierson lives with his parents:

How the spell of their magic changed the appearance of the house! The flowers looked out on sky and plain with meek, mauve-tinted eyes, after having absorbed all the amaranth of a cloudless night, the aureole of early morning, and a something, I know not what, that belongs to dreams and distance wafted on waves of colour from far-away places. At times the flowers imparted to the rugged logs the semblance of a funeral pyre, their beauty suggesting the mournful pomp of some martyr-queen, with pale, wondering eyes, awaiting the torch in a pallium of purple. They gave to the entrance a sort of halo that symbolised the eternal residuum of all things mortal and visible. (34)

Bray brilliantly unpacks the meaning of this strange paragraph, concentrating on the references to purple and the multiple meanings of "amaranth"—as humble wildflower, unfading flower of poetry, and the purple of the night sky. He sees the metaphor of the martyr-queen awaiting immolation in her "pallium of purple" as introducing death into the natural beauty of the morning glories. The paragraph thus encapsulates the meaning of the entire book, which Bray sees as exploring the Romantic archetypes of garden, apocalypse, and Lincoln: "For the question is bound to arise: why, if Illinois is Edenic, a natural paradise where man and the land are in harmony, is the supernatural and violent cleansing of the apocalypse necessary? The answer, fundamentally grounded in the Fall, is that the evil of proslavery thinking threatens to ruin the agrarian commonwealth" (40). This is an ingenious and persuasive reading of both paragraph and book, but it neglects the oddest feature of the paragraph: the relation between setting and image. Granted that Grierson wants to introduce the theme of death into his idyllic setting, how does he manage to transform a log house into an oriental funeral pyre, humble Illinois morning glories into a martyr-queen, and the entire scene into a halo symbolizing "the eternal residuum of all things mortal and visible"?

The Illinois landscape in Grierson is no longer the Romantic prairie of Bryant and Farnham, in which a mighty external nature acts on the receptive, perceiving individual, but a symbolist prairie, in which nature has been subsumed by the perceiving self and internalized as emblematic of human experience. What Richard Ellmann has written of another symbolist, William Butler Yeats, is equally true of Yeats's contemporary Grierson: "Wordsworth's new theme was a renewal of man's bond to nature; Yeats's was the uncovering of a second nature in which all outward things took their character from being internalized. The mighty presence which for Wordsworth was outside man was for Yeats inside, and all the scenic elements, such as stars, sea, winds, and woods, became emblematic of human activities" (108).

Bernard DeVoto insists that *The Valley of Shadows* is not fiction but an act of memory. "Purely as a psychological feat," he writes, "it is amazing. When [Grierson] was past fifty he began a systematic, ten-years labor, forcing his memory to reproduce what as a child he had seen and heard and felt, had been terrified and exalted by—and what he had come to understand was of tremendous import—in the Sangamon country" (xiii). DeVoto's interpretation of Grierson's work as a feat of memory is only partially credible. *The Valley of Shadows* gives the impression not so much of a reproduction of childhood experience as of a fresh creation built around some scraps of childhood memories. The mingling of memory and meditation finds expression in a marked oscillation in Grierson's discourse between two styles, one rather plain and even earthy, the other extraordinarily lush and evocative. The morning glory passage, for example, is introduced straightforwardly: "One day, after breakfast, my attention was arrested by a sight which gave me a thrill of admiration. The morning glories were in bloom!" (33). This external fact established, Grierson moves into the interpretation of the flowers as martyr-queen and as a halo symbolizing "the eternal residuum of all things mortal and visible."

The effect of this rush from the external world of phenomena into the self is not to interpret the outside world but to annihilate it. "There is a law of correspondence," Grierson writes, "a kind of secret code proper for each condition of life, and people become distorted and confused when this law is ignored" (31). But Grierson does not treat the correspondence between nature and the self as a balanced one. When log cabins become oriental funeral pyres and morning glories become martyr-queens, the link between the objective and the subjective is stretched so far that it snaps, and the result is, as Ellmann puts it, not an interplay between nature and the self but a second, internalized nature, emblematic only of human activities.

The recurring action in *The Valley of Shadows* is this sort of devouring of nature, in which a natural scene is briefly presented and then internalized into an inner, "mystic" landscape. This process ordinarily occurs in the passages that Grierson calls "silences." "In looking back," he writes, "I have come to the conclusion that the power displayed by the most influential preachers and politicians of the *ante-bellum* days in Illinois was a power emanating from the spiritual side of life, and I have done my best to depict the 'silences' that belonged to the prairies, for out of those silences came the voices of preacher and prophet and a host of workers and heroes in the great War of Secession" (xxix). The morning glory passage is one such silence; a more extended one is a description of the prairie sky in chapter 6, "The Cabin of Socrates." Grierson and his father have gone to visit Zack Caverly. Two other neighbors drop by, and after some commonplace conversation, they go outdoors and sit in silence, looking at the sky:

> An unparalleled radiance illumined the prairie in front of the cabin; the atmosphere vibrated with a strange, mysterious glow; and as the eye looked upward it seemed as if the earth was moving slowly towards the stars.
>
> The sky resembled a phantasmagoria as seen from the summit of some far and fabulous Eden. The Milky Way spread across the zenith like a confluence of celestial altars flecked with myriads of gleaming tapers, and countless orbs rose out of the luminous veil like fleecy spires tipped with the blaze of opal and sapphire.
>
> The great stellar clusters appeared like beacons on the shore of infinite worlds, and night was the window from which the soul looked out on eternity.
>
> The august splendor of the heavens, the atmosphere, palpitating with the presence of the All-ruling Spirit, diffused a feeling of an inscrutable

power reaching out from the starry depths, enveloping the whole world in mystery.

I sat and gazed in awe and silence. (62–63)

This passage, like the morning glory one, reveals a remarkable confusion of the natural and the cultural, or perhaps not so much a confusion as a systematic conversion of the natural into the artificial. The Milky Way becomes "a confluence of celestial altars flecked with myriads of gleaming tapers," the stars are "fleecy spires tipped with the blaze of opal and sapphire," and night itself becomes a "window." Like the morning glory passage, in which "a something, I know not what, that belongs to dreams and distance wafted on waves of colour from far-away places," the sky passage is full of evocations of the mysterious and ineffable: the atmosphere vibrates with "a strange, mysterious glow," and the sky diffuses "a feeling of an inscrutable power," "enveloping the whole world in mystery."

Grierson's strange, internalized representation of the landscape of "the Lincoln country, 1858–1863," seems to invite an aesthetic reading, in which the reader, like the young Grierson gazing at the night sky, reacts with "awe and silence." *The Valley of Shadows* is far from ideologically neutral though; Grierson's representations of the Illinois prairie express his central ideas, which his biographer briskly sums up in this way: "that an old order has been replaced by a vulgar and materialistic democracy; that a new era of mystical art is slowly being born; that ultimate truth is spiritual; and that intuition and feeling lead to this truth" (Simonson 106). The two voices of old man and little boy in *The Valley of Shadows* bespeak a larger division in Grierson's vision of history, between a time when the world was perceived as suffused with spiritual meaning and the present, when realism and democracy seem to have driven all splendor from the world. *The Valley of Shadows* is a deeply reactionary book, in the most literal sense, a reaction to a troubled modern world by withdrawal into an idealized past and a landscape pervaded by spirit, its reality erased and replaced by a wholly internalized alternative nature.

The prairie had taken its place in the American imagination by the middle of the nineteenth century, and it is significant that in Grierson's book it appears as memory, as nostalgic dream. But the prairie survives in Illinois, tamed and fenced, and is still available as a symbol. George F. Will, for example, in assessing Ronald Reagan's career, can write whimsically, "The remarkable flatness of the prairie suggests that God had good times in mind—smooth infields for countless baseball diamonds—when he designed Illinois, where Ronald Reagan spent his formative years. There Reagan acquired a talent for happiness" (13). The fine Illinois writer Richard Powers can set a crucial scene in his 1988 novel *Prisoner's Dilemma* on the Illinois prairie, with its "minimalist architecture of the straight row, bare box, and spare headland" (164), and have it mean to his characters very much what it meant to prairie travelers two hundred years earlier. Rachel and her brother Artie, worried about their father's mysterious illness, are driving in a battered Pinto from Dekalb to Chicago:

> Outside, the last, sourceless light scattered across vacancy, running unopposed all the way to the horizon. Another stunted sob came from Rach's throat and she burst a laugh. She looked, eyes liquid, at her brother, unable to add to the unmitigated Illinois landscape with anything so small as words. They were surrounded by an endless, fenceless detention camp of openness where nothing—not rage, not native contrarity, not even their father's final illness—could ruffle this Euclidian perfection. (171–72)

As garden, desert, and "endless, fenceless detention camp of openness," the Illinois prairie has been permanently implanted in the American imaginative landscape.

2

Writing Lincoln

The figure of Lincoln is as overpowering a presence in Illinois discourse as the prairie is, both in popular culture (one can stay at the Abe Lincoln Motel and eat an Abeburger, at least in Springfield) and in the work of Illinois poets, novelists, and playwrights. The stream of Lincoln interpretation began even before his death and became a torrent after the assassination, in the rush to record memories of the fallen hero. By the end of the nineteenth century, the memory of Lincoln had become a permanent presence in Illinois and formed an important theme in the flowering of Illinois writing we call (rather inaccurately) the Chicago Renaissance. Lincoln, or at least Lincoln as he came to be read, figured in Jane Addams's attempt to reshape American social thought and in Vachel Lindsay's, Edgar Lee Masters's, and Carl Sandburg's attempts to reshape American poetry. Lindsay grew up in a house associated with Lincoln, and his presence, shadowy and idealized, pervades Lindsay's poetry, culminating in "Abraham Lincoln Walks at Midnight." "Lincoln" was, for Edgar Lee Masters, the site of a violent personal inner battle. He veered between contributing to the sentimentalized Lincoln (in the Ann Rutledge epitaph in *Spoon River Anthology*, for example) and placing a demonized Lincoln against an idealized Stephen A. Douglas in a projection of his curiously polarized view of American culture (most notably in his scandalous 1931 biography, *Lincoln: The Man*). Sandburg's preoccupation with Lincoln is legendary; it pervades his poetry and culminates in his six-volume romantic biography *Abraham Lincoln: The Prairie Years and the War Years.* Lincoln is as readily available to contemporary writers. In Mark Costello's much reprinted story "Murphy's Xmas," for example, the action shapes itself silently around the progress of Lincoln's funeral train to Springfield. In William Maxwell's *So Long, See You Tomorrow,* set in Lincoln, Illinois, the life and death of Lincoln are a constant parallel to the action of the novel. Even in Saul Bellow's wry, ironic *Humboldt's Gift,* recurring references to Lincoln provide a surprising, unexpected standard against which a debased, materialistic contemporary culture is measured.

The representation of Lincoln in Illinois writing is, of course, a minor outcropping in the mountain of Lincoln literature, and it can hardly be understood except in the context of that mountain. That context is riddled with the most violent conflicts and contradictions. The central issue in Lincoln studies is most often stated as a conflict between romance and reality, between subjective idealizations or debasements of Lincoln and objective historical accounts. The goal of professional Lincoln historians has been to recover the real Lincoln of history as opposed to the mythic Lincoln of the popular imagination. This is quite understandable, and it would be hard to imagine any responsible historian having any other goal. But even a cursory, selective reading of the Lincoln literature suggests that a simple division between reality and myth is not very illuminating—or even possible. Rather than a simple binary, we find a crowded continuum, from bare, factual chronicle at one end to the wildest fancies at the other. Furthermore, these many voices seem in continual conflict. The supposedly most straightforward issues seem unresolvable: the influence of the frontier on Lincoln, his views on race, the nature of his marriage, his conduct of the Civil War. In 1936, the Lincoln historian James G. Randall asked, "Is the Lincoln theme exhausted?" The answer, predictably, was that it was not. Nor is it more than half a century later, nor is it likely to be. The whole point seems to be its inexhaustibility; "the Lincoln theme" seems to be the historian's version of a perpetual-motion machine, forever generating discourse, never reaching resolution or consensus.

Such an extraordinary situation suggests that "Lincoln" has come to be less a real figure in history than a site for cultural debate, an empty space for the staging of conflicts over the interpretation of American life, an analogue, on a vastly larger scale, of the prairie as a field of projection of conflicting values. In the prairie, Americans encountered the American Other, a landscape utterly unlike those of Europe or the eastern United States and for which new cultural categories had to be constructed. The essential "mysteriousness" persistently attributed to the figure of Lincoln perhaps suggests that he, too, is an American Other, a "new" man who cannot be fitted into familiar characterological categories. Ralph Waldo Emerson, Walt Whitman, and Nathaniel Hawthorne, along with many other of his contemporaries, saw him in this way. As he has receded into the past and has been buried by the endless commentaries, he has lost none of his power to attract controversies that touch the quick of basic issues in American life: the significance of the Civil War, the meaning of the reconceptualization of America from the Republic to Lincoln's semimystical Union, the place of regionalism within a hegemonic national culture, and many others.

That such issues are still with us is demonstrated by the paper war that broke out upon the publication in 1984 of Gore Vidal's *Lincoln: A Novel.* The book was initially greeted by excellent reviews. In perhaps the most influential one, Harold Bloom wrote in the *New York Review of Books,* "No biographer, and until now no novelist, has had the precision of imagination to show us a plausible and human Lincoln, of us and yet beyond us. Vidal, with this book, has done just that, and more: he gives us the tragedy of American political history, with its most authentic tragic hero at the center, which is to say, at our center" (5). In the longest and the most laudatory review, in *Encounter,* Owen Dudley Edwards, the dean of Irish historians, wrote, "It is brilliant, moving, thoughtful. . . . It raises important questions about historical matters, and its quality invites any disagreement about its arguments and suggestions to prove itself likewise constructive" (33).

There were dissenting voices, but there was nothing in the initial reviews that foreshadowed the furious attack leveled against the book by American Lincoln historians beginning about a year later. At the annual symposium of the Abraham Lincoln Association, Roy P. Basler, a literary historian, called it "among the worst novels I have ever read." "More than half the book," Basler said, "could never have happened as told," and "another 25 percent of the book is made up of episodes that might have happened, but never as they are told by Vidal" (1985:10).

Richard N. Current, author of *The Lincoln Nobody Knows,* took up the rod next in the *Journal of Southern History,* calling Vidal's *Lincoln* "a potpourri of his own inventions and bits and pieces he has picked up from other authors." "Vidal," he wrote, "is wrong on big as well as little matters. He grossly distorts Lincoln's character and role in history by picturing him as ignorant of economics, disregardful of the Constitution, and unconcerned with the rights of blacks" (81). There were similar attacks on Vidal by Stephen B. Oates, author of a popular life of Lincoln, and by the distinguished southern historian C. Vann Woodward.

Vidal, of course, was not the man to take this lying down, and he replied to his critics in a pointed "Exchange" in the *New York Review of Books.* He took some time to debate factual points, but he directed his strongest attack on the academic historians' assumptions that they have exclusive access to historical "truth" and that such truth is ideologically neutral. "Current," he wrote, "has fallen prey to the scholar-squirrels' delusion that there is a final Truth revealed only to the tenured few in their footnote maze; in this he is simply naive. All we have is a mass of more or less agreed-upon facts about the illustrious dead and each generation tends to rearrange those facts according to what the times require" (56).

There were other entries in the debate over the historicity of Vidal's novel, but the debate was brought to a close, in a sense, in a wise article by the eminent Lincoln scholar Don E. Fehrenbacher, in which, after reviewing the novel as history, he concluded:

> Fiction and nonfiction are arbitrary categories. On the one hand, most fiction is written about the real world; that is why so many first novels are quasi-autobiographies. On the other hand, there is a fictional element in all historical narrative, and even in analytical writing there is a point beyond which inference takes on the quality of fiction. Neither the historical Lincoln nor the fictional Lincoln is the totally "real" Lincoln. Both are constructs of factual materials shaped and cemented with imagination. (245)

The heat in the debate over Vidal's *Lincoln* was generated not by the friction between good history and bad history but between two different views of what history is, between the realist position held by Basler, Current, et al. and the nominalist position held by Vidal and Fehrenbacher. The former would claim that historical writing can and should capture reality; the latter claim that there is an inevitable gap between history as event and history as text. (The Vidal tempest in a teapot is not, of course, the only place where these issues have been debated; it was merely a highly visible reflection of an ongoing reassessment of historiography in the work of such figures as Roland Barthes, Hayden White, and Paul Ricoeur.)

The view that both historical and fictional Lincolns are "constructs of factual materials shaped and cemented with imagination" has implications not just for the historian and novelist but for the reader as well. It can free us from the crude and inaccurate dichotomy between "reality" and "myth" and empower us to read in a genuinely historical way, locating all our texts, whether historical or fictional, within the historical situations within which they were written and recognizing the cultural work each performed in its particular time and place.

All these generalizations about Lincoln discourse in general apply also to the small part of it that is our subject: the developing use, within Illinois writing, of Lincoln as a synecdoche for the state. The five writers included—William H. Herndon, Jane Addams, Vachel Lindsay, Edgar Lee Masters, and Carl Sandburg—represented Lincoln in various genres—memoir, essay, poems, and biographies of dubious historicity—but all will be read similarly, as "constructs of factual materials shaped and cemented with imagination" or, alternatively, as "more or less agreed-upon facts" arranged "according to what the times require." The representation is partial, of course—a synecdoche of a synecdoche—but it may suggest the process by which Lincoln has come to represent, among many other things, Illinois.

Herndoniana

The tendency to divide Lincoln narratives into the "realistic" and the "mythic" began very early. It underlay the first quarter-century of Lincoln biography and reached an early culmination in the critical storm that raged over the publication in 1889 of the most famous and influential of the early biographies, *Herndon's Lincoln: The True Story of a Great Life* by William H. Herndon and Jesse William Weik. Herndon, Lincoln's Springfield law partner, began planning his biography shortly after Lincoln's death and collected a great deal of material through interviews and correspondence with Lincoln's associates, material that he eventually had bound in three thick volumes as his "Lincoln Record." His attempts to write a life of Lincoln based on these materials, however, continually foundered until 1881, when he met Jesse Weik, who prodded him into action and eventually wrote the final draft of the biography, based on Herndon's letters and rough drafts.

During the years between 1865 and 1889, however, the biographers had not been idle. Henry J. Raymond had published *The Life and Public Services of Abraham Lincoln* as early as 1865, followed almost immediately by Josiah G. Holland's substantial idealization *The Life of Abraham Lincoln* and Isaac Arnold's equally sentimental *History of Abraham Lincoln and the Overthrow of American Slavery,* both in 1866. During these early years, though, there were strong rumors that the materials for a sharply differing view of Lincoln's life and character lay buried in Herndon's "Record," rumors which Herndon fueled in interviews and in his series of Springfield lectures on such topics as Lincoln's presumed romance with Ann Rutledge, his marriage, and his general character. An 1872 *Life of Abraham Lincoln,* published under the name of Lincoln's close associate Ward Hill Lamon (but actually ghostwritten by Chauncey F. Black) and largely based on Herndon's materials, was greeted with widespread revulsion for its unsavory contents and its debunking tone.

By 1889, then, Lincoln biographies were already being divided into the mythic and the realistic, with proponents of the mythic appealing to canons of propriety, patriotism, and moral inspiration and such advocates of reality as Lamon and Black upholding the claim of truthfulness over that of inspiration. Herndon made his long-delayed entry vehemently on the side of realism. "If the story of [Lincoln's] life," he wrote in his preface, "is truthfully and courageously told—nothing colored or suppressed; nothing false either written or suggested—the reader will see and feel the presence of the living man. He will, in fact, live with him and be moved to think and act with him. If, on the other hand, the story is colored or the facts in any degree suppressed, the reader will be not only misled, but imposed upon as well. At last the truth will come, and no man need hope to evade it" (vii-viii).

Herndon's Lincoln is a fascinating book, and its complex and ironic representation of Lincoln is bracing after the saccharine hagiographies of Holland and Arnold. But is it any "truer" than the hagi-ographies? Objections to the book when it first appeared centered on its alleged impropriety; later historians have questioned its accuracy. Herndon's most dubious contribution to Lincoln biography was the Ann Rutledge myth, the assertion that Lincoln had a passionate romance with Ann Rutledge of New Salem that shaped his entire subsequent life. A close second is his interpretation of Lincoln's marriage, the belief that Mary Todd, stung and embittered by being left at the altar on January 1, 1841, devoted her life, after the marriage finally took place, to revenge by making Lincoln's home a domestic hell. Both these issues—and others, such as Herndon's representation of Lincoln's father as lazy and shiftless and his vehement insistence that Lincoln was a religious skeptic—involve not so much matters of fact as interpretation. There really was an Ann Rutledge whom Lincoln knew, and there was obviously discord in the Lincoln home, but Herndon's conclusions drawn from these facts are shaky and unconvincing.

There is enough "myth," in other words, in this "realistic" account for Herndon's best and most sympathetic critic, David Herbert Donald, to conclude, "Now that Herndon's manuscripts are available to the historian, his life of Lincoln must more and more be evaluated as literature rather than as biography" (367). But what does it mean to evaluate a biography as "literature"? Donald shrewdly points out that Herndon's Lincoln is quite as mythic as the idealized Lincoln of Holland and Arnold. If Holland's account of a prettified perfect man constituted an eastern Lincoln myth, Herndon's representation of a brawling, canny frontier hero constituted a western Lincoln myth: "It is a mistake to consider these two main streams of tradition as representing respectively the 'ideal' and the 'real' Lincoln. Each was legendary in character. The conflict in Lincoln biography between the Holland-Hay-Tarbell school and the Herndon-Lamon-Weik contingent was not essentially a battle over factual differences; it was more like a religious war. One school portrayed a mythological patron saint; the other, an equally mythological frontier hero" (372).

Donald's myth-and-symbol interpretation of Herndon's Lincoln is persuasive; however, there is more in Herndon than mythmaking, and his Lincoln is more than just a Mike Fink or a Davy Crockett. If Lincoln in Herndon's pages is often a representative frontier joker, he is even more often a distinctly unrepresentative, secretive intellectual with extraordinary powers of "slow, cold, clear, and exact" thought (591) and great force of will, which enabled him to wait for the right moment and then act "with the unerring aim and power of a bolt from heaven" (609).

Herndon's Lincoln is also complicated by Herndon's ambivalent treatment of Lincoln's Illinois background and its significance both for Lincoln and for the national culture. Herndon's western myth of Lincoln is only the most superficial manifestation of a theme that runs throughout the book: the relation between Lincoln and his early environment and its significance for understanding his place in history. Herndon begins his book by declaring that the story of Lincoln is the story of a miraculous rise from the worst of origins:

> Many of our great men and our statesmen, it is true, have been self-made, rising gradually through struggles to the topmost round of the ladder; but Lincoln rose from a lower depth than any of them—from a stagnant, putrid pool, like the gas which, set on fire by its own energy and self-combustible nature, rises in jets, blazing, clear, and bright. I should be remiss in my duty if I did not throw the light on this part of the picture, so that the world may realize what marvellous contrast one phase of his life presents to another. (ix-x)

The "marvellous contrast" between Lincoln's early life and his later triumph is a recurring challenge to biographers. Did Lincoln become the man he was in spite of his frontier experiences or because of them? The eastern answer, from Josiah Holland to Stephen B. Oates, is that Lincoln overcame the cultural barrenness and deprivation of the frontier to become a heroic American. The western answer, stated most fully and romantically in Carl Sandburg, is that the frontier made Lincoln, that his character was an expression of positive frontier values rather than a transcending of negative ones.

Herndon is ambivalent on the issue. He begins by unequivocally identifying Lincoln's frontier environment as a "stagnant, putrid pool" and repeats the point several times in the early chapters. "It will always be a matter of wonder to the American people, I have no doubt—as it has been to me," he writes in chapter 2, for example, "that from such restricted and unpromising opportunities in early life, Mr. Lincoln grew into the great man he was" (41–42). But as the book goes on and Herndon warms to his subject, frontier Illinois is presented more and more positively, and explicit connections are drawn between Lincoln's environment and his character. The

Clary's Grove boys, for example, are rude and rough, and "yet place before them a poor man who needed their aid, a lame or sick man, a defenceless woman, a widow, or an orphaned child, they melted into sympathy and charity at once" (82). They exemplify "that firm and generous attachment found alone on the frontier—that bond, closer than the affinity of blood, which becomes stronger as danger approaches death" (95). The Illinois bar of Lincoln's day was a rough-and-ready affair, and yet it was the crucible that forged Lincoln's power of reasoning: "this rude civilization crystallized both his logic and his wit for use in another day" (312). Herndon's Illinois is a civilization in the making: "The vigor and enterprise of New England fusing with the illusory prestige of Kentucky and Virginia was fast forming a new civilization to spread over the prairies!" (164). By the end of the book, Lincoln is not an inexplicable product of a putrid pool but an understandable, if extraordinary, product of a vital, developing new civilization. If this theme is tentative, ambivalent, and only gradually unfolding, it mirrors Herndon's own apparent uncertainty and the tentative, developing character of the frontier culture he describes.

The structure of *Herndon's Lincoln* suggests Herndon's struggle to define the meaning of his friend's life against the background of American history. That structure is, as one might expect from the complex, collaborative history of composition, rather casual and even ungainly. Of the book's twenty chapters, the first five trace Lincoln's childhood and youth in Kentucky, Indiana, and Illinois. Chapter 6 is devoted to a detailed, rather melodramatic account of his presumed love affair with Ann Rutledge, and chapter 7 covers his tragicomic association with Mary Owens. Six more chapters are devoted to Lincoln's mature life as a Springfield lawyer up to the eve of his nomination for the presidency. In chapter 14, Herndon pauses for a general characterization of the mature Lincoln, touching on his marriage, practicality, superstitiousness, fatalistic philosophy, and attitude toward religion. Three chapters cover his nomination, election, and inauguration as president and his habitual routine as president. Chapter 18 is wholly devoted to statements about Lincoln's character from Joshua Speed and Leonard Swett. The Civil War is covered in one short chapter, with an account of the assassination written by Gertrude Garrison. The book concludes with a chapter based on Herndon's 1866 lecture on Lincoln's character.

Such a structure is obviously less than satisfactory for a full biography of Lincoln. The extreme compression of the account of Lincoln's presidency and the Civil War unbalances the book. As Donald comments, "*Herndon's Lincoln,* for all practical purposes, stops with 1861. It is a statue without a head" (353). On the other hand, by devoting almost all of his book to the Illinois Lincoln, Herndon is obviously playing to his own strength. We read *Herndon's Lincoln* not for a balanced account of Lincoln's entire life but for the testimony of Herndon and those from Kentucky, Indiana, and Illinois who knew Lincoln and from whom Herndon took statements.

Herndon's Lincoln may be a badly made book, but it is obviously a made one; thoughout we see Herndon struggling to make his materials form a coherent narrative, and his occasional clumsiness in doing so makes the process even more visible. In one passage, while describing Lincoln's methods as a lawyer, Herndon writes, "He thought slowly and acted slowly; he must needs have time to analyze all the facts in a case and wind them into a connected story" (337). The passage is self-referential: Herndon, too, is analyzing all the facts in the case and trying to "wind them into a connected story." Indeed, the book is organized like a trial, with a series of witnesses, voices from Herndon's "Record," passing through the pages and with Herndon's voice breaking through to sum up Lincoln's character in a last chapter that reads like a summing-up to a jury.

Winding facts into a connected story requires, on the basic level, what Hayden White has usefully called emplotment, the decision, in constructing a story, of what sort of shape the story will have. There are four possibilities, if we agree with White, following Northrop Frye, to let the deciding factor be the power of the protagonist: romance, in which the protagonist is powerful throughout; irony, in which the protagonist is powerless throughout; tragedy, in which the protagonist moves from power to powerlessness; and comedy, in which the protagonist moves from powerlessness to power. It might be objected that the shape of Lincoln's life is not a literary choice but a fact of history. Stories, however, do not appear "naturally" and "inevitably" in history; they are cultural constructs used to order the infinitely complex and essentially meaningless flux of events. "No given set of casually recorded historical events can in itself constitute a story," White writes; "the most it might offer to the historian are story elements. The events are made into a story by the suppression or subordination of certain of them and the highlighting of others, by characterization, motific repetition, variation of tone and point of view, alternative descriptive strategies, and the like—in short all of the techniques that we would normally expect to find in the emplotment of a novel or a play" (1978:84).

In emplotting, in winding all the facts into a connected story, the biographer's hand is not completely free, any more than the lawyer's is. It would be difficult, obviously, to emplot Lincoln's presidency as a comedy. Yet his early life, with its movement from obscurity to power and fame and its wealth of comic anecdote, lends itself easily to comic emplotment. This is the choice Herndon makes; by concentrating on Lincoln's Illinois years and subordinating the presidential years (and even assigning the assassination to another writer), Herndon is able to shape Lincoln's life into a consistent movement from powerlessness to power, with the tragedy of the war and the assassination reduced almost to an afterthought.

Herndon's comic Lincoln is for the most part a western folk hero, immensely strong and yet inveterately lazy, a spinner of yarns and a practical jokester, a romantic lover of Ann Rutledge and yet a comically henpecked husband to Mary Todd, a study, as Herndon said, in western character, the "original western and south-western pioneer—the type of . . . open, candid, sincere, energetic, spontaneous, trusting, tolerant, brave and generous man" (quoted in Donald 371).

Yet there is much more than the comic folk hero to Herndon's Lincoln. The portrait is darkened and enriched by Herndon's own presence in the book. Historical facts become a coherent story not only by being arranged in a familiar shape but also by being presented from a particular point of view and narrated by a voice that is always able to stop to comment, explain, and interpret. This voice is conventionally repressed in history and biography and regarded as a neutral medium for the presentation of the subject. To read a biography as "literature" requires attention to the narrative voice as well as to the subject. In the case of *Herndon's Lincoln,* it is not difficult to give this attention; Herndon himself demands it. A secondary subject of *Herndon's Lincoln* is Herndon's Herndon, as Donald points out (350).

The Herndon of *Herndon's Lincoln* appears in multiple guises, according to the nature of the narrative situation. He is divided between the young man of the time of the action and the old man of the time of the writing. The Herndon of the time of the action, Herndon as character, is a rather minor, self-effacing figure. He slips into the action in the middle of chapter 4 as part of the crowd watching the *Talisman* steamboat try to descend the Sangamon River, with Lincoln one of the men clearing the way of overhanging branches from the shore (87). He reenters in chapter 8, when Lincoln moves to Springfield and Herndon becomes "warmly attached" to him: "There was something in his tall and angular frame, his ill-fitting garments, honest face, and lively humor that imprinted his individuality on my affection and regard. What impression I made on him I had no means of knowing till many years afterward. He was my senior by nine years, and I looked up to him, naturally enough, as my superior in everything—a thing I continued to do till the end of his days" (181). The law partnership is formed in chapter 9, and Herndon appears subsequently as a minor character, often as a silent observer, in a number of scenes, culminating in the warm scene of Lincoln's departure from the law office for the White House (482–85) and the briefer account of Herndon's last visit with Lincoln in Washington (506–8).

The Herndon of the time of composition is anything but self-effacing. His style in itself is distinctive enough to keep him constantly in our minds. "I wrote," he told a correspondent, "in a gallop—with a whoop" (quoted in Donald 363), and, even as tidied up by Weik, his style is energetic and exuberant. His own comments on Lincoln's style are perhaps unconsciously revealing:

> His language indicated oddity and originality of vision as well as expression. Words and language are but the counterparts of the idea—the other half of the idea; they are but the stinging, hot, leaden bullets that drop from the mould; in a rifle, with powder stuffed behind them and fire applied, they are an embodied force resistlessly pursuing their object. In the search for words Mr. Lincoln was often at a loss. He was often perplexed to give proper expression to his ideas; first, because he was not master of the English language; and secondly, because there were, in the vast store of words, so few that contained the exact coloring, power, and shape of his ideas. This will account for the frequent resort by him to the use of stories, maxims, and jokes in which to clothe his ideas, that they might be comprehended. (592–93)

This may or may not be a good assessment of Lincoln's use of language, but it is certainly a very good example of Herndon's: the startling, sweeping judgment that our most eloquent president was "not master of the English language," the unexpected metaphor of words as bullets, "resistlessly pursuing their object," and the general "oddity and originality" of expression.

In this passage, as throughout the book, Herndon stands in a complexly complementary relation to his subject. Lincoln is in most respects everything that Herndon is not; he is Herndon's Other, a longtime partner who nevertheless was "so different in many respects from any other one I ever met before or since his time that I cannot say I comprehended him" (585). Herndon is quick, Lincoln is slow; Herndon is impetuous, Lincoln is deliberate; and most of all, Herndon is a romantic radical, Lincoln a conservative rationalist. In one of the most amusing passages in the book, and another unconsciously self-revealing one, Herndon reports describing Niagara Falls to Lincoln:

> As I warmed up with the subject my descriptive powers expanded accordingly. The mad rush of water, the roar, the rapids, and the rainbow furnished me with an abundance of material for a stirring and impressive picture. The recollection of the gigantic and awe-inspiring scene stimulated my exuberant powers to the highest pitch. After well-nigh exhausting myself in the effort I turned to Lincoln for his opinion. "What," I inquired, "made the deepest impression on you when you stood in the presence of the great natural wonder?" I shall never forget his answer, because it in a very characteristic way illustrates how he looked at everything. "The thing that struck me most forcibly when I saw the Falls," he responded, "was, where in the world did all that water come from?" (297)

Herndon's conclusion from this absurd little scene is, "He had no eye for the magnificence and grandeur of the scene, for the rapids, the mist, the angry waters, and the roar of the whirlpool, but his mind, working in its accustomed channel, heedless of beauty or awe, followed irresistibly back to the first cause" (297). The point is not only that Herndon doesn't get the joke of Lincoln's comically deflating line but also that he chooses to dramatize himself as the enthusiast and Lincoln as the logician and then proceeds to generalize about Lincoln on the basis of a misapprehension. Here, as often in the book, the reader is forced to agree with Lincoln: "Billy, you're too rampant" (362–63).

Lincoln is more than Other to Herndon though; identification, as well as polarization, is at work in the relationship. The qualities he emphasizes in Lincoln—opposition to slavery, powers of analysis, intuitive sympathy with the masses of the people—are clearly ones that he attributes to himself as well. Perhaps the most sweeping connection is their common culture on the frontier. Herndon, after all, was also a product of that "stagnant, putrid pool" and was faced with a similar challenge to transcend or transform it. The significant image here is perhaps the dingy, littered Lincoln-Herndon law office, with the latest issues of the *"Westminster* and *Edinburgh Review* and a number of other English periodicals," to which Herndon subscribed, lying on the table (436). The impulse behind those subscriptions and behind Herndon's restless book-buying was perhaps a need to locate obscure, cultureless little Springfield in relation to the larger world of English and eastern culture. *Herndon's Lincoln* is itself a last attempt to achieve respectability, if not greatness, after a life of obscurity and failure.

All these dynamics are working in the passages of diagesis in the book, those in which Herndon suspends his narrative to turn directly toward the reader to explain, analyze, and interpret. The most extensive of these passages is the famous last chapter, in which Herndon undertakes to generalize about Lincoln's character. This chapter contains some of the most memorable passages in the book—those in which he minutely describes Lincoln's appearance and mannerisms—and some of the most dubious—those in which he undertakes to analyze Lincoln's psychology. Herndon's purpose is to establish that Lincoln was "the central figure of our national history" and "the sublime type of our civilization" (611), but in the process he makes some startling judgments, especially in regard to the interplay of reason and emotion in Lincoln's personality:

> Mr. Lincoln's perceptions were slow, cold, clear, and exact. Everything came to him in its precise shape and color. To some men the world of matter and of man comes ornamented with beauty, life, and action; and hence more or less false and inexact. . . . He was not impulsive, fanciful, or imaginative; but cold, calm, and precise. He threw his whole mental light around the object, and, after a time, substance and quality stood apart, form and color took their appropriate places, and all was clear and exact in his mind. His fault, if any, was that he saw things less than they really were; less beautiful and more frigid. He crushed the unreal, the inexact, the hollow, and the sham. He saw things in rigidity rather than

in vital action. He saw what no man could dispute, but he failed to see what might have been seen. (591)

This is an interesting but unconvincing analysis, even in the light of Herndon's own text. The Lincoln who almost killed himself for love of Ann Rutledge and who as president could not refuse a petition for clemency seems very remote from this icy figure. Whatever personal work such a passage performed for Herndon, who presents himself as a man to whom the world did come "ornamented with beauty, life, and action," it certainly performed cultural work as well. By the end of the book, the chaotic and disorderly Illinois frontier has produced the most disciplined and rational of men, a man outside the pattern of traditional culture but who is nevertheless "the sublime type of our civilization."

The antithesis of chaos and control appears also in another "literary" feature of *Herndon's Lincoln,* its figuration, or use of metonymy and metaphor. The book, perhaps even more than most biographies, is heavily metonymic: details are connected by contiguity rather than similarity. Herndon's great asset, his "Record," was also something of a liability; too much redundant or irrelevant material is included merely because Herndon has a document. The book has a loose, serial construction. The scrapbook structure is countered, however, to some degree by a few governing metaphors, the overwhelmingly most important of which is water.

The metaphor is introduced in the preface with the representation of the frontier as a "stagnant, putrid pool" and Lincoln as a pocket of swamp gas "which, set on fire by its own energy and self-combustible nature, rises in jets, blazing, clear, and bright" (ix). The key statement of the metaphor, though, comes with Lincoln's arrival in New Salem: "He assured those with whom he came in contact that he was a piece of floating driftwood; that after the winter of deep snow, he had come down the river with the freshet; borne along by the swelling waters, and aimlessly floating about, he had accidentally lodged at New Salem" (79). This metaphor sticks in Herndon's mind and is introduced repeatedly throughout the book. When his employer Denton Offut leaves New Salem, Lincoln finds himself a piece of "floating driftwood" again (92). The dissolution of the Whig party leaves Lincoln, "though proverbially slow in his movements, prepared to find a firm footing when the great rush of waters should come and the maddening freshet sweep former landmarks out of sight" (381). Lincoln finds himself "drifting about with the disorganized elements that floated together after the angry political waters had subsided" (382). Herndon returns to the metaphor for the ending of his book:

> This long, bony, sad man floated down the Sangamon river in a frail canoe in the spring of 1831. Like a piece of driftwood he lodged at last, without a history, strange, penniless, and alone. In sight of the capital of Illinois, in the fatigue of daily toil he struggled for the necessaries of life. Thirty years later this same peculiar man left the Sangamon river, backed by friends, by power, by the patriotic prayers of millions of people, to be the ruler of the greatest nation in the world. (610)

The recurring metaphor of water might be regarded as merely ornamental if it did not, with its emphasis on floods, freshets, and drifting, tap so clearly into Herndon's preoccupations with Lincoln's character (and perhaps his own). Central among these is will versus aimlessness. From being a piece of floating driftwood Lincoln became a force whose will shaped the nation's history. Upon what resources, in himself and in his culture, did he draw for this transformation? How did Lincoln achieve such purposeful control over his own and the nation's destiny, while Herndon continued to drift, unable even to finish his book? The long-delayed writing of *Herndon's Lincoln* is both a tribute to that mystery and an attempt to rewrite Herndon's own personal narrative, to give it a happy ending.

Herndon's Lincoln is a distinctively Illinois Lincoln, not only in the material Herndon furnished for a mythic frontier comic hero but also for his exploration of deeper, paradoxical links between Lincoln and the stagnant pool out of which he rose. His Lincoln, sometimes almost indistinguishable from himself, is a mysterious figure who was, like himself, of the frontier but also, unlike himself, somehow beyond it.

Jane Addams's Lincoln: The "Rustic American Inside"

To move from *Herndon's Lincoln* to Jane Addams's "Influence of Lincoln," the second chapter of her autobiographical *Twenty Years at Hull-House* (1910), is to move from one extreme of Lincoln representation to another. Addams's brief essay, barely eleven pages long, makes no claim to give us the "real Lincoln." It is merely a series of seemingly random memories loosely associated with Lincoln and concluding, rather primly, that Lincoln's importance is that he "made plain, once for all, that democratic government, associated as it is with all the mistakes and shortcomings of the common people, still remains the most valuable contribution America has made to the moral life of the world" (26). The interesting aspect of Addams's essay is not this conclusion but the chain of thoughts, memories, and associations which leads up to it and which it inadequately summarizes. In "Influence of Lincoln," we can observe on a miniature scale, as in *Herndon's Lincoln* on a vastly larger one, the conversion of Lincoln into "Lincoln," the historical fact into meaning.

This meaning, despite the rather predictable conclusion, is quite personal to Addams. Her representation of Lincoln, like Herndon's, is a complex negotiation between author and subject. The difference is that Addams is highly self-conscious about this negotiation and even makes it the subject of her meditation (admittedly easier to do if you are not attempting an objective biography). It is an overstatement in most cases to say that those who write about Lincoln end up writing about themselves; it is not in the case of Addams, who frankly acknowledges that she is tracing back to its origins the bit of Lincoln that has become part of herself.

The project of the first five chapters of *Twenty Years at Hull-House* is to perform this sort of personal archaeology of Addams's own mind as, at the watershed age of fifty, she looks back on her life. These first chapters are not conventionally autobiographical; names, dates, and major events in Addams's early life are suppressed in favor of a loosely lyrical series of often trivial memories linked by association rather than by strict logic or chronology. Addams is a diffident memoirist; her goal is not self-aggrandizement but illumination of the pattern of thought and feeling that led to the founding of Hull-House. "The earlier chapters," she writes in her preface, "present influences and personal motives with a detail which will be quite unpardonable if they fail to make clear the personality upon whom various social and industrial movements reacted during a period of twenty years" (2). After the introductory chapters on the thirty years before Hull-House, Addams largely effaces her own presence in a series of chapters on aspects of Hull-House activities.

The brief spiritual autobiography that opens *Twenty Years at Hull-House* strongly emphasizes the evolution of an ethic of service. The first chapter is largely devoted to Addams's memories of her father, a Quaker miller in Cedarville, Illinois. John Huy Addams's personal creed is "mental integrity above everything else" (10), a creed Addams adopts as her own, however much its individualistic emphasis may be broadened and enriched in her later life. (The book is dedicated "to the memory of my father.") After the chapter on Lincoln, Addams moves on to "Boarding-School Ideals," an account of her college years at Rockford Female Seminary, whose atmosphere of suffocating idealism left her "absolutely at sea so far as any moral purpose was concerned" and with only "the desire to live in a really living world" to buoy her up (39). A fourth chapter, "The Snare of Preparation," deals with her travels through Europe, where she experiences feelings of uselessness that established the "subjective necessity for social settlements" (68). It culminates in the famous bullfight episode, in which, filled with self-revulsion at having complacently watched a brutal bullfight, numbed by a romanticizing aestheticism, she resolves to return to Chicago and establish a settlement house. A fifth chapter tells of the "First Days at Hull-House."

The first five chapters of *Twenty Years at Hull-House* present five stages in Addams's moral development, and yet it is easier to say what these stages are not than what they are, since Addams proceeds by a *via negativa*. The action of the five chapters is a successive stripping away of received ethical values to the point where Addams can move into Hull-House "without any preconceived social theories or economic views" (2). The ethics of Hull-House are not Addams's father's "mental integrity above everything else" (though that principle is subsumed in them), not the reaction to the British class system that underlay the English settlement movement, not Rockford's "rose-colored mist" (39) of idealism, and, above all, not the religion of culture expressed in the European Grand Tour. The ethical foundation of Hull-House was not a principle or a system but an action, a verb: "to live in an industrial district of Chicago" (2).

It is in this context that Addams considers the "Influence of Lincoln." She begins with the memory of Lincoln's death: "Although I was but four and a half years old when Lincoln died, I distinctly remember the day when I found on our two white gate posts American flags companioned with black. I tumbled down on the harsh gravel walk in my eager rush into the house to inquire what they were 'there for.' To my amazement I found my father in tears, something that I had never seen before, having assumed, as all children do, that grown-up people never cried" (15). As Addams looks back, she sees the death of Lincoln as marking a crucial stage in her childhood development, a widening of her awareness from the family home to the larger world; it was "my initiation, my baptism, as it were, into the thrilling and solemn interests of a world lying outside the two white gate posts" (15).

The initiation into the larger world is primarily an initiation into the pervasiveness of meaningless suffering and loss: Lincoln's assassination, the lingering death of a local boy wounded in the war, and the accidental shooting of a boy who was the sole survivor of five brothers in the war. Addams remembers her first childish perceptions of "that grief of things as they are, so much more mysterious and intolerable than those griefs which we think dimly to trace to man's own wrongdoing" (17).

If Lincoln's death marks Addams's youthful initiation into the "mysterious injustice" (17) of life, his memory also, paradoxically, provides a means of comfort against that despair, a point made with characteristic obliqueness in an account of a family trip to Madison, Wisconsin, to see Old Abe, the eagle that was the mascot of the Eighth Wisconsin Regiment during the Civil War and was then kept in the rotunda of the state capitol. Old Abe is something of a disappointment, with his veteran attendant ready to tell of all thirty-six battles Abe had survived. Addams nevertheless experiences an epiphanic moment, not when she sees the eagle but when she lifts her eyes to the rim of the capitol dome, carved with two friezes of "soldiers marching to death for freedom's sake" and of "pioneers streaming westward" (18). The vision of common people, combined with "the image of the eagle in the corridor below and Lincoln himself as an epitome of all that was great and good," makes a greater impression than the attendant's factual history, proving to an older, reminiscing Addams that "children are as quick to catch the meaning of a symbol as they are unaccountably slow to understand the real world about them" (18).

This vision of Lincoln as symbol of both the "grief of things as they are" and "all that was great and good" is inextricably entangled with the memory of her father, who kept in his desk a packet of letters from Lincoln, all beginning "My dear Double-D'ed Addams," and two pictures of Lincoln hanging in his room. It is no wonder that, as Addams writes, "I always tend to associate Lincoln with the tenderest thoughts of my father" (20).

Father and Lincoln alternate almost interchangeably in the reminiscences that follow, some drawn from her childhood and others from her more recent history at Hull-House. She remembers drawing comfort from the statue of Lincoln in Chicago's Lincoln Park during the 1894 Pullman strike, as she had once drawn comfort from the images of Lincoln in her father's room. She remembers a tribute to her father at the time of his death to the effect that he was the only member of the Illinois legislature whose reputation was so high that he had never even been offered a bribe and her own shame later when a group of Chicago businessmen offered her a contribution if she would stop lobbying for a sweatshop bill. She remembers meeting some of Lincoln's contemporaries at an Old Settlers' Day at which her father spoke and, as a result, losing interest in Thomas Carlyle's *Heroes and Hero Worship,* which she had intended to give to young people at Hull-House, and giving them instead Carl Schurz's *Appreciation of Abraham Lincoln.*

For the mature Addams of Hull-House, Lincoln is a model of achievement sprung from common roots:

> We were often distressed by the children of immigrant parents who were ashamed of the pit whence they were digged, who repudiated the language and customs of their elders, and counted themselves successful as they were able to ignore the past. Whenever I held up Lincoln for their admiration as the greatest American, I invariably pointed out his marvelous power to retain and utilize past experiences; that he never forgot how the plain people in Sangamon County thought and felt when he himself had moved to town; that this habit was the foundation for his marvelous capacity for growth; that during those distracting years in Washington it enabled him to make clear beyond denial to the American people themselves, the goal towards which they were moving. (23)

Addams's emphasis on Lincoln's low beginnings and the heights to which he rose is commonplace; it is the same contrast that fascinated Herndon. In context, however, the passage is deeply personal. She herself was a country Illinoisan who had "moved to town," she is at the moment pausing at the height of her fame as a national leader to look back on her childhood as a frail, motherless child in Cedarville, and she knows that her power comes from knowing how "the plain people" thought and felt. It is not that Addams is cultivating her own myth by a covert comparison with Lincoln; rather, she is concerned to show that Hull-House sprang from peculiarly American, and even specifically Illinoisan, values.

"Influence of Lincoln," like *Twenty Years at Hull-House* as a whole, is full of contrasted pairings, as is perhaps inevitable in an account of change and development. There is not only Lincoln's humble past and his glorious apotheosis but also the innocent Jane before the assassination and the experienced Jane after that initiation into sorrow. Lincoln himself is Janus-faced, emblem of both "the grief of things as they are" and "all that was great and good." The common people in the Wisconsin frieze are contrasted with a vision of high individualistic heroism; the stainless elder Addams is contrasted with his daughter, guilty of being offered a bribe; and Thomas Carlyle's European heroes are contrasted with Carl Schurz's American one.

These doublings come to a head in the extended account of a trip to England, which concludes the chapter and forms its climax. At a conference in Oxford on the settlement movement, Addams is increasingly uncomfortable with the English rationale for settlements, which seems largely a reaction to the English class system. "However inevitable these processes might be for class-conscious Englishmen," she writes, "they could not but seem artificial to a western American who had been born in a rural community where the early pioneer life had made social distinctions impossible. . . . I found myself assenting to what was shown me only with that part of my consciousness which had been formed by reading of English social movements, while at the same time the rustic American inside looked on in detached comment" (24).

Addams thus develops "an uncomfortable sense of playing two roles at once" (24), and it is "almost with a dual consciousness" that she goes to visit Edward Caird, Master of Balliol College. Suddenly she remembers that Caird has lectured on Lincoln:

> The memory of Lincoln, the mention of his name, came like a refreshing breeze from off the prairie, blowing aside all the scholarly implications in which I had become so reluctantly involved, and as the philosopher spoke of the great American "who was content merely to dig the channels through which the moral life of his countrymen might flow," I was gradually able to make a natural connection between this intellectual

penetration at Oxford and the moral perception which is always necessary for the discovery of new methods by which to minister to human
needs. (25)

Like most of Addams's stories, this one begins in conflict and ends
in reconciliation, through the recognition of a "natural connection."
It is the memory of Lincoln that supplies that connection between
Chicago and Oxford, between the prairie and the study, between
moral perception and intellectual penetration.

All of the chapter up to this point—the memory of the death of
Lincoln, Old Abe the war eagle and the dome of the state capitol,
Lincoln's letters to her father, the immigrants at Hull-House—has
been devoted to constructing that part of Addams's identity that is
the skeptical "rustic American inside." That aspect of autobiography by which a self is constructed through memory and narrative is
very visible here. (Only our willing complicity in this process would
allow us to accept that Lincoln's death would make a four-and-a-
half-year-old think of "that which Walter Pater calls 'the inexplicable
shortcoming or misadventure on the part of life itself'" [17].) Not
only is Addams constructing her self in "Influence of Lincoln" but
she is constructing a Lincoln as well, a Lincoln made up of scraps
of history, memories of her father, and her own needs. It is not the
"real" Lincoln, nor does it pretend to be. It is one of the many Lincolns that were written into American selves and American culture
in the years after his death.

The Lincolns of the Prairie Poets

If Jane Addams, in Chicago in 1910, felt that writing about
Lincoln was a way of locating her Hull-House project within American culture, even specifically midwestern, Illinois culture, many of
her contemporaries were of the same mind. At almost exactly the
same time, three poets from small-town Illinois were embarking
on careers devoted, in very different ways, to sweeping critiques
of American culture. All three—Vachel Lindsay, Edgar Lee Masters, and Carl Sandburg—gave Lincoln an important place, either
positively or negatively, within their representations of America.

In the narrative ordinarily told about American poetry, Lindsay,
Masters, and Sandburg occupy a minor place near the beginning of
The Coming of Modernism. According to this narrative, in the years

just before World War I, the wandering star of literary history hung briefly over Chicago, where Illinois poets were writing interesting protomodern poems. It then moved on to London, where T. S. Eliot and Ezra Pound produced fully realized modernist poems, and then back to America, where it paused over Wallace Stevens, William Carlos Williams, and their heirs, while Lindsay, Masters, and Sandburg returned to the noncanonical darkness whence they had come. Recent critiques of canonization in American literature have called this simple narrative into question. Cary Nelson, for example, has recently written that

> when literature is provisionally contextualized—both within its own broader history and within American social history as a whole—some of the more well-known failures in modern poetry become as interesting as the established successes, and some nearly forgotten poets become genuinely exciting again. Indeed, we need to stop thinking of artistic failure as a statement only about individual tragedy or the weaknesses and limitations of individual character and begin to see it as culturally driven, as a complex reflection of social and historical contradictions, as the result of the risks of decisions made in a network of determinations. In that context Vachel Lindsay's (1879–1931) doomed fantasy of a fully public and participatory democratic poetry becomes, say, as important to our sense of the culture as T. S. Eliot's virtually decisive co-optation of modernism in *The Waste Land.* (69)

Lindsay, Masters, and Sandburg are all "interesting" and sometimes even "exciting" failures in Nelson's sense. They thought big: all three aimed, perhaps anachronistically, at large-scale interpretations of American life, and if their reach exceeded their grasp, that was a function of their ambitions as much as their artistic limitations. Their work had little to do with modernism, as it is usually defined, despite their rejection of genteelism. They pursued, in their own ways, the Whitmanesque goal of a democratic poetry into an age whose complexities and contradictions continually undercut that goal and instead seemed to demand a fragmentary, ironized poetry directed at an increasingly narrow audience. Lindsay, Masters, and Sandburg were not so much precursors of that movement as the last stand against it.

Lindsay, Masters, and Sandburg were not "regional" poets in the ordinary sense; all three aspired to national significance. But all three drew their primary material from their small-town Illinois backgrounds, and inevitably Lincoln was an important part of it. Perhaps less inevitably, for at least Masters and Sandburg, the figure of Lincoln came to be a field of contention where they fought out their deepest convictions, a screen on which they projected their own values. If the result was not very happy for the historical understanding of Lincoln, it is instructive as an example of how Lincoln has been assigned meanings often remote from the historical record.

Despite Harriet Monroe's description of Lindsay as "from Lincoln's own country, a poet of Lincoln's own breed" (quoted in Ruggles 207), Lincoln appears comparatively seldom as a principal subject in Lindsay's poetry. As Ann Massa writes, "Lincoln escaped over-emphasis because he was a perpetual, implicit part of Lindsay's Springfield. His overt role in Lindsay's writings was effective for its brevity and memorable for its intensity" (161). One stanza is devoted to Lincoln in "Litany of the Heroes":

> Would I might rouse the Lincoln in you all,
> That which is gendered in the wilderness
> From lonely prairies and God's tenderness.
> Imperial soul, star of a weedy stream,
> Born where the ghosts of buffaloes still gleam,
> Whose spirit hoof-beats storm above his grave,
> Above that breast of earth and prairie-fire—
> Fire that freed the slave.
>
> (1984–86, 2:440)

Lindsay's major representation of Lincoln in his poetry is "Abraham Lincoln Walks at Midnight," in which he imagines Lincoln walking the streets of Springfield after the outbreak of World War I, grieving at the continued violence of nations:

> It is portentous, and a thing of state
> That here at midnight, in our little town
> A mourning figure walks, and will not rest,
> Near the old court-house pacing up and down,
>
> . . . .
>
> A bronzed, lank man! His suit of ancient black,
> A famous high top-hat and plain worn shawl
> Make him the quaint great figure that men love,
> The prairie-lawyer, master of us all.
>
> . . . .
>
> It breaks his heart that kings must murder still,
> That all his hours of travail here for men

Seem yet in vain. And who will bring white peace
That he may sleep upon his hill again?
(1984–86, 1:239–40)

Eleanor Ruggles, Lindsay's biographer, tells an instructive story of the composition of "Abraham Lincoln Walks at Midnight." Lindsay's collection *The Congo and Other Poems* was in press at Macmillan when war broke out in 1914. He asked the publisher if he might add some poems about the war to the collection. Told that he might, he wrote drafts of "Abraham Lincoln Walks at Midnight" and five other poems in twenty-four hours. The next day, he took the manuscript of "Abraham Lincoln Walks at Midnight" to the home of his friend Mary Humphrey:

> He didn't know how to dress Lincoln, he told her, except for a top hat and black suit. Did Lincoln have a cane?
> No. A long coat? No, what Mr. Lincoln wore, said Mary, was what her father the Judge remembered older men of the period as wearing—a shawl or small afghan around his shoulders, and she waited long enough to see Vachel sit on the porch railing and write the shawl in:
> > His suit of ancient black,
> > A famous high top-hat and plain worn shawl. . . .
> > (231)

It seems inconceivable that Lindsay, surrounded by images of Lincoln all his life and a graphic artist himself, should have so little visual memory of Lincoln. Clearly what he wanted from Mary Humphrey was a typical, instantly recognizable image of Lincoln, not a fresh or unexpected one. Lincoln, in both "Litany of the Heroes" and "Abraham Lincoln Walks at Midnight," is not so much a person as an icon, an instantly recognizable symbol triggering certain associations.

Lindsay had no gift for, and apparently no interest in, either characterization or narrative. In none of his poems does he attempt to draw a realistic character or tell a well-developed story. (He attempts both in the prose *Handy Guide for Beggars* and *Adventures While Preaching the Gospel of Beauty,* but even here the characters tend to be generalized types—the "dog-man," the "Man Under the Yoke"—and the narratives diarylike strings of short anecdotes. See 1988, 1:1–81, 153–210.) "Litany of the Heroes" is structured like a static frieze, listing twenty-nine heroes, from Amenophis the Fourth to Woodrow Wilson, in as many stanzas, and giving only a sketchy, idealized description of each. (And indeed Lindsay did draw twenty-six large panels for the poem, which he would arrange as a frieze around the room when he expounded the poem. See 1925:xlvi–xlvii.) The eight lines devoted to Lincoln, exactly the same number that the other twenty-eight heroes receive, sketch in a prairie Lincoln, above whose grave ghostly buffalo hooves beat and who draws on the mystic powers of air, water, earth, and fire: the "star of a weedy stream," the "breast of earth and prairie-fire." The Lincoln of "Abraham Lincoln Walks at Midnight" is equally dematerialized, a presence made up of little more than his iconic clothing—suit, hat, and shawl—and memories of Hamlet's father (he "stalks until the dawn-stars burn away") and of Christ (he "carries on his shawl-wrapped shoulders now / The bitterness, the folly and the pain").

Lindsay was interested in Egyptian hieroglyphics, as many of his predecessors in American poetry were (see Irwin). In "Adventures While Singing These Songs," the foreword to his 1923 *Collected Poems,* he wrote, "Unless I am much mistaken, I shall sooner or later evolve a special type of United States Hieroglyphics, based on a contemplation of the borderline between letters and art, and the bridges that cross it" (1925:17–18). Two years later, the preface to the revised edition had become "Adventures While Preaching Hieroglyphic Sermons," and almost the entire preface is given over to hieroglyphics. Lindsay sometimes seems to mean by *hieroglyphics* the wispy, fanciful drawings that accompany some of the poems. He describes, for example, submitting the "hieroglyphic" "The Shield of Lucifer" to Susan Wilcox, his high school English teacher, and then reading the accompanying poem, "Lucifer," over and over to her for her criticism and revision. (The hieroglyphic and poem are reprinted in 1925:110–18.) At other times, he seems to think of the hieroglyphics as mental, rather than literal, images: "These ideas I have had so long, I necessarily see them as pictures in the air. . . . Still they are with me in fancy, perhaps five hundred hieroglyphics, big and little, all of them differing from one another and all of them differing from anything that I have ever been advertised in the newspapers as doing" (1925:xxiii). Lindsay seems to think of these hieroglyphics not merely as ideas for poems but also as units in a comprehensive system of meaning:

I believe that civic ecstasy can be so splendid, so unutterably afire, continuing and increasing with such apocalyptic zeal, that the whole visible fabric of the world can be changed. I believe in a change in the actual fabric, not a vague new outline. Therefore I begin with the hieroglyphic, the minute single cell of our thought, the very definite alphabet with which we are to spell out the first sentence of our great new vision. And I say: change not the mass, but change the fabric of your own soul and your own visions, and you change all. (1925:xxvi)

There is much that is fuzzy here, but it is such passages as this that lead Marc Chénetier to see Lindsay's poetry as fundamentally semiotic rather than oratorical in intention: an attempt to build up, sememe by sememe, a renewed, democratic consciousness for America. Ann Massa agrees, citing Lindsay's comment that the rapidity of America's growth had left the American mind "an overgrown forest of unorganized pictures" (1925:xxii) and his hope that he could produce "a new language, integrating the visual and the mental processes, [that] could clarify a muddled America for muddled Americans" (Massa 257). Massa, however, considers Lindsay's "United States Hieroglyphics" a failure, since Lindsay never succeeded in producing hieroglyphic pictures that could communicate complex messages without accompanying verbal texts. What if, though, the texts themselves are regarded as hieroglyphic, as Lindsay sometimes seems to suggest, networks of discrete verbal pictures that are somewhat more than literal and somewhat less than symbolic, hieroglyphics intended to organize the "unorganized pictures" of the American mind? Lindsay's representations of Lincoln, at any rate, seem to work in this way; shallow stereotypes in isolation, they take on whatever meaning they have as parts of a large system of American symbols.

Edgar Lee Masters could not stomach Lindsay's poems about Lincoln. In his 1935 biography of Lindsay, he wrote, "Without historical perceptions, and unconscious of the meaning of the war, and unmindful of who it was that waged it, and to what end, [Lindsay] celebrated its central figure, Lincoln, as if Lincoln were the chief figure of the pioneers, and the fellow of the Virginia heroes. History was never more misvalued; no great song more compelled to rest upon itself without assistance from the truth" (258). Yet in his earlier years Masters himself had written a number of poems idealizing Lincoln to the point of sentimentality. What had happened?

Masters, up until about 1920, accepted and even contributed to the idealization of Lincoln current in small-town Illinois. Looking back from the perspective of 1936, he wrote in his autobiography *Across Spoon River:*

> At that time [1893] I had an admiration for Lincoln, even believing the falsehood that the War Between the States was inevitable and the result of an irrepressible conflict, though my grandfather, who knew Lincoln there in the Petersburg-New Salem country, had given me the materials for a very different judgment of Lincoln. But at this time I followed on after the mythmaking that was being carried on in histories, biographies and poems. The Gettysburg Address was a miracle worker not to be stayed. (172)

Three of the *Spoon River* (1916) epitaphs are devoted to historical associates of Lincoln, and they are uniformly idealizing. Hannah Armstrong, with whom Lincoln boarded at New Salem, recalls going to Washington during the war to get a discharge for her sick son Doug,

> And when he saw me he broke in a laugh,
> And dropped his business as president,
> And wrote in his own hand Doug's discharge,
> Talking the while of the early days,
> And telling stories.
>
> (229)

William H. Herndon's epitaph presents him as an old man dreaming of his past association with Lincoln:

> And I saw a man arise from the soil like a fabled giant
> And throw himself over a deathless destiny,
> Master of great armies, head of the republic,
> Bringing together into a dithyramb of recreative song
> The epic hopes of a people.
>
> (224)

And most famously (and sentimentally) Ann Rutledge speaks from the grave:

> Out of me unworthy and unknown
> The vibrations of deathless music;
> "With malice toward none, with charity for all. . . ."
> I am Anne Rutledge who sleep beneath these weeds,
> Beloved in life of Abraham Lincoln,

> Wedded to him, not through union,
> But through separation.
> Bloom forever, O Republic,
> From the dust of my bosom!
>
> (220)

(Fifteen years later, Masters, in *Lincoln: The Man* [1931], not only was skeptical about the Ann Rutledge legend but also attacked the Second Inaugural as "triple distilled Hebrew curses, its myrrh mixed with honey and gall" [454], and even attacked Lincoln for not giving Ann a proper tombstone [49].)

Masters's growing antipathy to Lincoln can be traced through the 1920s. In *Mitch Miller* (1920), Lincoln is represented as affirmatively as he is in *Spoon River Anthology*. Near the end of the novel, Mr. Miller, Mitch's father, takes Skeet and Mitch to Lincoln's tomb for moral exhortation:

> . . . I can see for ages and ages the face of Lincoln on books, on coins, on monuments; until some day his face will be the symbol of the United States of America, when the United States of America has rotted into the manure piles of history with Tyre and Babylon, as it will if it doesn't turn back and be what Lincoln was: a man who worked and thought, and whose idea was to have a free field, just laws, and a democracy where to make a man not make a dollar is the first consideration. (232–33)

The tide began to turn in *Children of the Market Place* (1922), Masters's fictionalized account of the career of Stephen A. Douglas. Although Lincoln is presented favorably for the most part, it is clear that he represents the opposite of what he represented in *Mitch Miller*. He is the spokesman for "the market place," Masters's term for the Hamiltonian tradition of northern, urban commercialism opposed by Douglas, spokesman for the Jeffersonian tradition of southern, rural agrarianism.

This opposition hardened into dogma in Masters's succeeding books. *Lee,* Masters's "dramatic poem" of 1926, pits an idealized Robert E. Lee against an uncouth, Hamiltonian Lincoln:

> What matter if his rise was from the ranks,
> What the log cabin, and the river trails,
> As a youth he was for privilege and the banks
> Now fortressed by a block-house of fence rails.
>
> (10)

In another stilted, anachronistic "dramatic poem," *Jack Kelso* (1928), the aged Kelso gazes at a bronze statue of Lincoln and soliloquizes:

> Never in farthest fancies did you dream
> When we two wandered, fished and read together
> That you in bronze would look upon a scheme
> Of steel and stone, war's creature from its nether
> Foundations to its towers that rise and task
> This city and this nation, O Son of Iron,
> And scion of the hand-forge—you the mask
> Of the Age of Steel, whose meshes now environ
> All liberty, all grace, so fastly snared.
> The central sovereignty which you declared
> Above the land, created by the states,
> But by some magic potion made their master,
> Has bred this soulless monster and these hates
> Whose hope is ever Liberty's disaster.
>
> (222)

By the time Masters wrote *Lincoln: The Man,* then, he had presented his demonized version of Lincoln in print a number of times; perhaps it had escaped particular notice because it had appeared in comparatively unreadable works.

It was otherwise with *Lincoln: The Man,* which was greeted with such outraged hostility that many bookstores refused to stock it, hostility that Masters had no doubt anticipated. Masters apparently first planned the book as a response to Sandburg's *Abraham Lincoln: The Prairie Years,* which had appeared in 1926, but the immediate impetus for *Lincoln: The Man* was Albert J. Beveridge's *Abraham Lincoln, 1809–1858,* published in 1928. John Wrenn and Margaret Wrenn have pointed out that Masters probably anticipated his own Lincoln book in a 1928 review of Beveridge's, in which he wrote of the need for "an analytical study of Lincoln . . . to reduce the enigmatic character of the man to its psychological elements. . . . It will require a mind of high and singular gifts to do this, but it . . . can be done by the right sort of genius" (quoted in Wrenn and Wrenn 104).

In *Lincoln the Man,* Masters is quite frank in acknowledging how closely he follows Beveridge in the factual record of Lincoln's life. But Beveridge, Masters thinks, did not interpret Lincoln: "Beveridge did not argue or interpret; he did not write from any point of view. He merely gathered from every quarter, by the most tireless industry, whatever facts about Lincoln could be found" (1).

Masters takes as his task the "interpretation" of Beveridge's facts: "As no new fact of moment about Lincoln can now be brought to light, the time has arrived when his apotheosis can be touched with the hand of rational analysis" (1).

Masters's other major source, as he also acknowledges, is Herndon's book, which he characteristically reads as a wholly negative characterization. "The many things in Herndon's work," Masters writes, "which put Lincoln in no favorable light have been confirmed by Beveridge's thoroughly authentic biography" (1).

Masters's notion that Beveridge "did not write from any point of view" was also Beveridge's own belief. Benjamin P. Thomas summarizes Beveridge's position:

> "Historical interpretation" was synonymous with "indolence, ignorance and egotism. It means," he affirmed, "that certain facts are missing: the author does not have the humility and industry to search for these facts and keep on searching until he finds them; but that, instead, he tells the reader what he thinks these facts would have meant if they had been as he imagines them to have been." Facts, properly arranged, interpret themselves, he claimed, though Professor Charles A. Beard pointed out that "The moment you say arrangement, you say interpretation." (246)

Masters was correct in praising Beveridge's command of facts; Beveridge made many fine contributions to the Lincoln record, especially in reviewing critically the Herndon-Weik papers and in tracing Lincoln's legislative career through the records of the Illinois legislature and Congress and through contemporary newspapers. Masters was wrong, however, in suggesting that Beveridge had no interpretation of Lincoln. The Lincoln that emerges from Beveridge's pages is very much in the negative tradition of Lincoln biography. Lincoln's father was an ignorant lout, the frontier was an environment of unrelieved desolation, Lincoln jilted Mary Todd on the "fatal first of January," all pretty much as Herndon had said. It is possible that Beveridge would have been able to construct a coherent narrative of Lincoln's life had he been able to finish the book, but he died when he had brought the story only through the Lincoln-Douglas debates of 1858. He did seem to glimpse the difficulty ahead in accounting for Lincoln's conduct of the presidency in terms of the crafty, unprincipled, opportunistic politician he had presented. "I shall, of course, find my hero on the highest peak of Mt. Everest," he wrote, "but I shall have to go through many a bog, gully, and chasm in the painful ascent before I at last reach him on the heights of glory" (quoted in Thomas 258).

Beveridge, then, was a congenial source for Masters, and Masters's "analysis of Lincoln's mind and character" (2) consists of little more than a redaction of Beveridge, interspersed with abuse of Lincoln. Masters's book is arranged like a court case (as were Herndon's and Beveridge's, lawyers all; the influence of legal structures on patterns of Lincoln biography might be a fruitful study). He can make an inquiry into Lincoln's mind and nature, he declares at the outset, "just as an argument may be advanced in a court proceeding when all the evidence touching a given matter has been adduced" (1).

Masters summarizes the case against Lincoln almost immediately, as if he were making an opening statement to a jury:

> As late as 1858 Lincoln was denying with all his might that he was an abolitionist; and he was avoiding, as if they were contagion, the contact of fanatics like Garrison and Giddings and Phillips. In a few years he was at the head of an army which was singing hymns of praise to John Brown, who had robbed and murdered under the inspiration of that religious zealotry which claims to divine the purposes of God, and, under the warrant of heaven, proceeds to execute them. The Democratic Party, broken by the incredible radicalism of Southern leaders, fell down in 1860, and was walked over by the mongrel breeds who knew nothing and cared nothing about liberty and constitutional government; when, by compromise that affected no principle of moment, Douglas would have been elected president and the war averted, at that time, and perhaps for good. After that, with an army at the command of centralists and fanatics, with that army carrying on to victory, supported by great wealth, which saw its chances of fortune in military success, and in the despotisms of reconstruction, there was nothing of strength left in the country to oppose the sordid imperialism which arrived to rule. (2–3)

Masters's Lincoln narrative follows the plot-shape that Northrop Frye identifies as sixth-phase tragedy, which features a villainous hero and offers an unrelieved spectacle of the defeat of goodness and the triumph of evil (222–23). The narrative voice is jeremiadical, lamenting the triumph of the "unlettered," "torpid," "crafty," and "undersexed" Lincoln (see, especially, 138–56) and the defeat of a wholly idealized Douglas. Masters's treatment of the Gettysburg Address is representative: "In Lincoln's case the subjugation of the South had to be smeared over with religion, it had to be made at one with the creed of Methodists and Baptists, with the whole rank and file of Calvinism, with the nauseating piety and the sadistic righteousness of America as a Christian nation, in order to conceal its purpose, in order to satisfy those who fought for the Lord, if they fought at all, that such was their battle at Gettysburg" (480). Lincoln-bashing can go no further.

Lindsay was profoundly shocked by *Lincoln: The Man*. When it appeared, he wrote to his wife, "Masters Life of Lincoln is just as awful as its traducers make out. His mind is good but his disposition is just plain sick. . . . He hates Sandburg. Therefore he writes a life of Lincoln that reads like rattle-snake venom. . . . The gist of the book: —is that:—*Lincoln was a sneak, without brains enough to grasp hair-splitting subtleties, therefore came the civil war, the trusts, the skyscrapers, the churches and the dry vote! Also the Racketeers and the Rockefellers!"* (1979:450–51). Lindsay never communicated his disapproval to Masters—they never met after 1926—but Masters acknowledged in his biography that *"Lincoln: The Man* offended [Lindsay] greatly" (1936:351).

Sandburg, too, was offended by the book, which was partially directed at his own Lincoln biography, but he held his peace, at least publicly. The only reference in his correspondence to the book is in a 1931 letter to William Townshend: "Very curious, it seems to be one of those books that people like to read, forget, and not have around the house. Masters and I were close friends at the time he wrote The Spoon River Anthology. I could do a book on phases and origins of his latest work. The only decent thing for me to do now is say nothing" (1968:277).

Sandburg's own life-long obsession with Lincoln is legendary and is memorialized in a story told by John Steinbeck. While Sandburg was working on *The War Years,* he lived on the eastern shore of Lake Michigan and took an exactly timed walk along the shore every morning. A group of practical-joker friends hired a Chicago actor to impersonate Lincoln and greet Sandburg one morning at a certain point in his walk. The actor reported that when Sandburg, deep in thought, looked up and saw him, bearded and in frock coat, stove-pipe hat, and shawl, he merely bowed and said, "Good morning, Mr. President" (Callahan 130).

Sandburg's major treatment of Lincoln was, of course, the six-volume biography, but he also wrote a handful of Lincoln poems, which may be compared to Lindsay's and Masters's. In *The People, Yes* (1936), Lincoln is the subject of Section 57: "Lincoln? He was a mystery in smoke and flags" (1970:521–25). *The People, Yes* is a book-length poem largely made up of found material—folk sayings, anecdotes, and quotations—which by a process of accretion, as it were, seems intended to express the spirit of the rather amorphously conceived "people." Bold, simplistic, and serial in construction, the book is analogous to the populist public murals of 1930s art.

The Lincoln section follows the pattern of the whole. It contains 156 lines, of which 107 are quotations from Lincoln. This material is held together by the loosest of structures: after a brief introduction, three sections, each introduced by a question: "Lincoln? was he a poet? / and did he write verses?" "Lincoln? was he a historian? / did he know mass chaos?" and "Lincoln? did he gather / the feel of the American dream / and see its kindred over the earth?" These topics function loosely as answers to an introductory question: "Which of the faiths and illusions of mankind / must I choose for my own sustaining light / to bring me beyond the present wilderness?"

The tone of Section 57 is open and indeterminate. The speaker's question about what light will guide him out of the wilderness parallels Lincoln's challenge: "He took the wheel in a lashing roaring hurricane. / And by what compass did he steer the course of the ship?" There is no clear answer to either question, only a series of quotations from which to draw one's own conclusions. The poem is structured not by theme but by a series of oppositions common in Sandburg: something insubstantial (smoke) versus something substantial (flags). The poem is thus full of opposed terms: hurricane/compass, no policy/policy, chaos/organization, the American dream/the American reality.

These oppositions have something in common with the rhetorical distinction between metonymy and metaphor, the centrifugal proliferation of detail and the centripetal unification through shared meaning. Metonymic "mass chaos" struggles against the control of metaphoric "organization." What the principle of organization is, other than the figure of Lincoln himself, is the "mystery in smoke and flags." We shall see the same rhetorical structures operating, on a vastly larger scale, in *The Prairie Years* and *The War Years*.

Sandburg's other major Lincoln poem is "The Long Shadow

of Lincoln: A Litany," delivered as the Phi Beta Kappa poem at
William and Mary College in 1944 (1970:635–37). One of Sandburg's finest poems, "The Long Shadow of Lincoln" is an elegy for
the dead of World War II. Lincoln is present by name only in the
title and in the epigraph, from the Message to Congress of December 1, 1862: "We can succeed only by concert. . . . The dogmas of
the quiet past are inadequate to the stormy present. The occasion
is piled high with difficulty, and we must rise with the occasion. As
our case is new so we must think anew and act anew. We must disenthrall ourselves. . . ." The entire poem is a development of the last
sentence, "We must disenthrall ourselves," which is repeated twice
within the poem.

The tone of the poem is public and oratorical, suited to a cere-
monial occasion, and the first half is structured around a series of
imperatives:

> Be sad, be cool, be kind,
> remembering those now dreamdust
> hallowed in the ruts and gullies,
> solemn bones under the smooth blue sea,
> faces warblown in a falling rain.
>
> . . . .
> Be a brother, if so can be.
>
> . . . .
> Make your wit a guard and cover.
> Sing low, sing high, sing wide.
>
> . . . .
> Weep if you must
> And weep open and shameless
> before these altars.

These imperatives, each the subject of a verse-paragraph, explore
possible responses to bereavement: sadness, detachment, kindness,
brotherliness, even music and laughter.

The second half of the poem turns to the familiar thought that
the dead have not died in vain, ringing variations on the phrase,
"There is dust alive," and at the climax of the poem, the shadow of
Lincoln appears to endorse the thought:

> There is dust alive.
> Out of a granite tomb,
> Out of a bronze sarcophagus,
> Loose from the stone and copper

> Steps a whitesmoke ghost
> Lifting an authoritative hand
> In the name of dreams worth dying for,
> In the name of men whose dust breathes
>   of those dreams so worth dying for,
>   what they did being past words,
>   beyond all smooth and easy telling.

The poem ends with repetitions, villanellelike, of earlier lines of the poem:

> Be sad, be kind, be cool.
>   .   .   .   .
> Sing low, sing high, sing wide.
> Make your wit a guard and cover.
> Let your laughter come free
> like a help and a brace of comfort.

> The earth laughs, the sun laughs
> over every wise harvest of man,
> over man, looking toward peace
> by the light of the hard old teaching:
>   "We must disenthrall ourselves."

The grave music of "The Long Shadow of Lincoln" gains weight through two intertextual references. The poem alludes to the Gettysburg Address, even more than to the 1862 Message to Congress. Sandburg stands in a position similar to Lincoln's, publicly commemorating, late in a war, the dead of that war. The progress of the thought is identical, from honor to the dead ("those who here gave their lives that that nation might live") to comfort from the belief that their death has meaning ("we here highly resolve that these dead shall not have died in vain") to purpose for the future: "we must disenthrall ourselves" ("a new birth of freedom").

"The Long Shadow of Lincoln" is also linked intertextually with Lindsay's "Abraham Lincoln Walks at Midnight." The context is similar: another great war demanding young people's blood. The central conceit is also the same: the appearance of Lincoln's shade as a silent commentator. Lindsay's theme is antiwar; Lincoln grieves that "kings must murder still." Sandburg's is elegiac; his Lincoln lifts "an authoritative hand / In the name of dreams worth dying for." The poem gains richness and depth from the echoes.

In the prairie poets' Lincoln poems, Lincoln is dematerialized into a shadowy presence, or, better, an absence, which the poets fill with their own agendas, whether to rebuild the image-bank of America, to chastise a degenerate age, or to celebrate the "mystery" of America's fate. It is otherwise in Sandburg's Lincoln biography, where Lincoln is nothing if not substantial.

Carl Sandburg's Lincoln

Stephen B. Oates has denied that Sandburg's *Abraham Lincoln: The Prairie Years and the War Years* is biography at all. It is instead, he says, "mythical art," an evocation of a mythological hero who embodies "what Americans have always considered their most noble traits—honesty, unpretentiousness, tolerance, hard work, a capacity to forgive, a compassion for the underdog, a clearsighted vision of what is right and what is wrong, a dedication to God and country, and an abiding concern for all" (16). Oates is far from the first to question Sandburg's treatment of Lincoln. Edmund Wilson, in a much-quoted line, called it "the cruellest thing that has happened to Lincoln since he was shot by Booth" (115). Benjamin Thomas, on the other hand, in his survey of Lincoln biographies, thought that Sandburg had captured "those soul qualities of Lincoln which documentary facts alone may not disclose" (310).[1]

Oates's questioning of the genre of Sandburg's book—biography or myth—had been anticipated, too. Sandburg himself was troubled by the question and was never quite able to answer it, as we can see if we trace the narrative of composition of the book through Sandburg's letters. *The Prairie Years* was originally planned as a comparatively short, one-volume book for children; it grew, in the writing, to two hefty volumes intended for an adult, though popular, audience. The Civil War was originally to be treated as a short coda to the story of Lincoln's life in Illinois, but by 1924 Sandburg realized that to do so would be "to really tack on another book, of different style" (1968:225). By the time *The Prairie Years* was published in 1926, Sandburg could write to a correspondent, "Whatever I may undertake in the way of a 'sequel' will not start for five years and may

---

1. For a rare sympathetic treatment of Sandburg's *Abraham Lincoln* by a contemporary historian, see Robert W. Johannsen's excellent essay.

be of so different an order that it won't be thought of as a sequel"
(1968:236).

If *The Prairie Years* swelled and changed shape during its composition, the expansions and metamorphoses of *The War Years* over the
eleven years that Sandburg was writing it were even more striking.
After giving up the idea of a short conclusion to *The Prairie Years,*
Sandburg planned first one volume, then two. By 1935, work on
the book had "stretched out unimaginably beyond what was first
planned" (1968:317). The manuscript then ran to 700,000 words,
and Sandburg thought he would require 200,000 more to finish it;
he actually wrote another half-million (1968:329, 366). Even on
the eve of publication, he was wondering if the book had any real
shape; he wrote to Alfred Harcourt, his publisher, "Sometimes I
look at this damned vast manuscript and it seems just a memorandum I made for my own use in connection with a long adventure
of reading, study and thought aimed at reaching into what actually went on in one terrific crisis—with occasional interpolations
of meditations, sometimes musical, having to do with any and all
human times" (1968:372). Surely Sandburg must have identified
with Washington Irving, whom he quotes early in the first volume.
Speaking of his work on a five-volume life of George Washington,
Irving said, "I have taken things to pieces and could not put them
together again" (1939, 1:26). Perhaps Sandburg's most telling characterization of his *Lincoln,* however, was his description of it as "a
sort of History and Old Testament of the United States, a joke almanac, prayer collect, and compendium of essential facts" (1968:221).

A long memorandum, an almanac, a compendium: Sandburg's
technique in *Lincoln* seems to be a rather uncritical amassing of Lincoln materials, a vast, extended metonymic structure not limited by
any central metaphor or even central idea, except the general one of
Lincoln. All that brings the book to an end is the death of Lincoln;
otherwise it seems as if it could go on forever.

The problem of assessing the status of Sandburg's great mass of
materials is complicated by his decision to include no documenta-
tion. As Victor Hicken has pointed out, what puzzled historians
when Sandburg's book appeared was "exactly where Sandburg had
found much of his material. . . . It was difficult . . . to prove Sandburg wrong in certain segments of his writing. No one knew where
to go to find proof of error" (105).

The answer to where Sandburg found his material seems to be "anywhere and everywhere." In reading the book, one is likely to recognize passages not only from such reliable sources as John Hay's diary but also from such dubious ones as the anonymous diary of A Public Man and even such fictionalized works as *The Valley of Shadows,* all incorporated as if they were of equal reliability. The twelve-page list of "Sources and Acknowledgments" included in the first volume of *The War Years* does nothing to remedy the situation; it is seriously incomplete and gives no indication of the source of any particular passage.

Sandburg seems to have emphasized inclusiveness at the expense of every other virtue. The account of the research and writing of *Abraham Lincoln* that runs through the relevant sections of *The Letters of Carl Sandburg* is like a lesson in how not to do history. From the thousands of Lincoln volumes stored in his workroom and in adjacent buildings, Sandburg would rip out the pages he wanted, classify them in labeled envelopes, and eventually pin them up above his typewriter to be paraphrased and included. Once used, the pages were discarded or stored haphazardly so that Sandburg himself had no way of verifying the source of a fact or a quotation except his own excellent but humanly imperfect memory. Hundreds of the gutted books were stored in an outbuilding at the Sandburg home in North Carolina, in a sort of bibliographical burying ground (see McJunkin 117).

Sandburg threw a great deal of material into his voracious hopper that is only tangentially related to Lincoln, if it is related at all, and the reader is likely to pause frequently, in the midst of some interminable catalogue of folk superstitions or a list of old jokes that Lincoln "might have told," to ask if "Lincoln" isn't just a pretext for a mammoth miscellaneous collection of Americana out of which some meaning is expected to emerge, almost on its own.

Despite its heterogeneous, throw-it-all-in character, Sandburg's *Lincoln* does have a shape. Or rather it has two shapes, for *The Prairie Years* and *The War Years* are separate works, conceptually and structurally; they are complementary rather than continuous, even in the one-volume edition in which Sandburg attempted to compress and combine them. By initially writing Lincoln's life only up to his departure from Illinois, Sandburg was able to avoid the problem of the congruence of beginnings and endings that plagues Lincoln biographers. *The Prairie Years* deals with the "Pre-Whiskers Lincoln," *The War Years* with the "Whiskers Lincoln" (1968:225), and the continuity between the two is largely left to the reader to perceive.

By confining himself in *The Prairie Years* to Lincoln's early life up to the presidency, Sandburg is able to emplot Lincoln's life as what Northrop Frye calls a "fourth-phase comedy." Fourth-phase comedy, near the center of the comic range, is comedy of "the green world," of which Shakespeare's romantic comedies, such as *A Midsummer Night's Dream* and *As You Like It,* are familiar examples. In such plots, the protagonist's movement from weakness to mastery, the movement common to all comedy, is embedded in a lush, fertile, dreamlike natural setting, and the protagonist's growth seems identical to the processes of nature itself. In green-world comedies, Frye writes, the plots are "assimilated to the ritual theme of the triumph of life and love over the waste land" (182). The female principle rules in such plots, and the heroine is often identified with the earth itself. Such plots are not necessarily merely escapist, Frye emphasizes; they illustrate, "as clearly as any *mythos* we have, the archetypal function of literature in visualizing the world of desire, not as an escape from 'reality,' but as the genuine form of the world that human life tries to imitate" (184).

The Illinois of *The Prairie Years* is Frye's green world; the book is a sustained Illinois pastoral, within which Lincoln matures almost as part of the natural landscape. Sandburg is the most extreme of those who have found Lincoln the natural product of his Illinois environment rather than an anomaly within it. The young Lincoln of *The Prairie Years* grows like a plant, a part of the natural world. "He was growing," Sandburg writes in a variation of a theme that recurs throughout the two volumes, "as inevitably as summer corn in Illinois loam, when its stalks thicken as it lifts ears heavier with juices, and longer with its dripping tassels of brown silk. Leaning at the porch-posts of a store to which fewer customers were coming, he was growing, in silence, as corn grows" (1:163). Sandburg's idealization of Lincoln is expressed not so much in the list of Sunday-school virtues that Oates enumerates as in the persistent identification of the young Lincoln with the earth. The mysteriousness at the heart of Lincoln's character that Sandburg emphasizes persistently is essentially the mystery of nature itself, perhaps embodied in Sandburg's haunting (and largely fictional) figure of the mysterious mother Nancy Hanks (1:23ff.).

Much of the immense bulk of *The Prairie Years* is thus given over to lengthy descriptions of nature. At each stage of his life, Lincoln is placed within a rich natural setting. As Lincoln floats in a canoe down the Sangamon River toward New Salem, for example, Sandburg pauses to imagine the scene: "Glimpses of landscape flitted by where the bee and dragonfly were going amid Indian pink and the bluebell and running wild rose. Red haw and the bitter fox-grape had intimations of all-time to come. Behind the bumblebees buzzing in the yellow dust of goldenrod leaves, and behind the streamers of haze around the river curves, were hints, almost statements, of a future to follow the present, the intertwining of hours to come with hours that are" (1:133). Such a passage seems largely decorative, a piece of "vivid" writing to bring the scene to realistic life, but it also serves a thematic function in suggesting a "natural time"—an "intertwining of hours to come with hours that are"—within which Lincoln's own development takes place.

Natural time and human time form a recurring opposition in Sandburg's nature descriptions. Here is part of his description, for example, of the landscape around the Knob Creek, Kentucky, farm where the Lincoln family lived for four years:

> Trees crowd up its slopes [Muldraugh's Hill's] with passionate footholds as though called by homes in the rocky soil; their climbings have covered sides and crests till they murmur, "You shall see no tall hills here unless you look at us." Caverns and ledges thrust their surprises of witchery and wizardry, of gnomes and passwords, or again of old-time intimations and analogues, memories of reckless rains leaving wave-prints to hint or say Muldraugh's Hill and the Knob Creek valley are old-timers in the making of the world, old-timers alongside of the two-footed little mover known as man. In the bottom lands the honeysuckle ranges with a strength nothing less than fierce; so deep are its roots that, unless torn away by the machines of man, the bees count on every year a boomer harvest of its honey-stuff; black and brown butterflies, spotted and streaked with scrolls and alphabets of unknown tongues from the world of wings—these come back every year to the honeysuckle. (1:22–23)

Behind the superficial personifications of this passage, in which trees are "passionate" and murmur things to the onlooker, lies a remarkably knotted tangle of the human and the nonhuman, culture and nature. Caverns and ledges recall witches, wizards, and gnomes, though only to the mind of the human observer who brings a burden of history to the natural scene. The honeysuckle's tenacious roots are pitted, potentially, against machines, and butterflies are little flying books, inscribed with the "scrolls and alphabets of unknown tongues." "Man," in this passage and throughout the book, is a "two-footed little mover" whose actions are set deep within a natural matrix, Muldraugh's Hill and the Knob Creek valley, "oldtimers in the making of the world" compared to johnny-come-lately humanity.

In the romance world of *The Prairie Years,* Lincoln's mysterious Otherness is a function of his identification with the slow rhythms of natural time and natural process. To "read" Lincoln is to "read" nature, to decipher nature's "scrolls and alphabets of unknown tongues."

The opposition of nature and culture, natural process and human process, in the Muldraugh's Hill passage is echoed on a large, structural level in the book by the balancing of passages of landscape description with passages of contemporary world events, within which Lincoln's own solitary, isolated maturation is also embedded. Sandburg called these "the moonlight chapters," which "sketch streams of American and world events that connect with the Lincoln fate" (1968:255). The first of these passages, for example, in chapter 10, is introduced with the seven-year-old Lincoln looking up at the moon and asking, "What do you see?" The moon reports looking down on the Napoleonic Wars, the immigration of eight million people to America, and the flow of migration from the East Coast into the West (34–37). The passage concludes, "Such were a few of the many, many things the moon might have told little Abe Lincoln, nearly eight years old, on a winter night in 1816 on Little Pigeon Creek, in the Buckhorn Valley, in southern Indiana—a high quarter moon with a white shine of thin frost on the long open spaces of the sky" (1:37).

Sandburg's landscape descriptions and the moonlight chapters locate his Lincoln between natural history and human history, a green world of innocence and a human world of bitter experience, an opposition inscribed even in this short passage, with its contrast between human time—"nearly eight years old, on a winter night in 1816"—and the long reaches of the moon's natural time. By Sandburg's account, Lincoln was a mystical figure who was nurtured in the innocent, natural world of the Illinois prairie while an unnatural, corrupted world of public history hurtled toward crisis and who emerged at the critical moment to turn that world back toward its natural destiny.

The Prairie Years, then, embodies the mythos of comedy, a narrative of spring and summer and of rising strength drawn from the natural world. *The War Years* is emplotted altogether differently. Even better than *The Prairie Years,* it fits Sandburg's description of his work as a miscellany: "joke almanac, prayer collect, and compendium of essential facts." In his foreword, Sandburg suggests the loose structural principle of the book: "If those who are gone who had their parts and role in [the Civil War] could be summoned back to tell of the gaps and discrepancies, they might give unexpected answers to questions. And many witnesses on being dug up and given speech might again be noncommittal as ever on this or that circumstance" (1:vii). *The War Years* is a chronological arrangement of voices from the past. Close to half of the text consists of quotations and introductions to quotations: a sometimes bewildering collage of voices drawn from all sorts of sources, some unknown, others known but dubious, but all given some degree of credence.

Despite its inclusive, encyclopedic structure, though, *The War Years* is held together by the figure of Lincoln, here emplotted not as the fourth-phase comic hero of *The Prairie Years* but as a third-phase tragic hero, a fully matured, masterful protagonist, whose success is emphasized. As Frye points out is true of many third-phase tragedies, Sandburg's account of the tragic, wartime Lincoln has a double movement, one toward disaster, the other toward triumph. Beowulf's fight with the dragon ends with his death, but in a countermovement the dying Beowulf frees his people and caps a life of heroic achievement (Frye 221); similarly, Lincoln moves toward a death that from a limited perspective is a defeat but from a larger one is a triumph and an apotheosis.

The tone of Sandburg's portrait of the Lincoln of the war years, despite the shape in which it is emplotted, is not mythically idealized. Lincoln is presented as the harassed victim of office-seekers, the frontier jokester with a sometimes deficient sense of occasion, and the ineffectual husband and father as often as he is portrayed as the heroic statesman and military strategist. Despite Sandburg's displacements in the direction of verisimilitude, the armature beneath his structure is the mythos of third-phase tragedy. Appropriately, nature description seldom appears, and when it does, it is of autum-

nal or wintery landscapes, as in many passages that describe the
sufferings of soldiers on the winter battlefields of the war. At Fort
Donelson, "before the fighting began a cold wind came, snow fell,
the roads froze, and in ten-above-zero weather men fired and loaded
their muskets, and in the night huddled and shivered, seeking fences,
brush, trees, logs, to keep off the wind. Neither side dared light a
bivouac fire. Men and boys were found next morning frozen stiff"
(1:461).

An occasional passage of springtime imagery contrasts with the
general sterility of the war and recalls the lush landscapes of *The
Prairie Years,* usually as a promise of the renewal of life after the trials
of the war years. Sandburg sets Lincoln's first inauguration, for example, thus: "Spring comes gently to Washington always. In early
March the green of the grass brightens, the magnolia softens. Elms
and chestnuts burgeon. Redbud and lilac carry on preparations soon
to bloom. The lovemaking and birthing in many sunny corners go
on no matter what or who the blueprints and personages behind
the discreet bureau and departmental walls" (1:120). The return of
life and fertility—"lovemaking and birthing"—after the holocaust
is also embodied in the figure of Liberty awaiting installation atop
the unfinished Capitol: "On the slopes of lawn fronting the Capitol building stood a bronze statue of Liberty shaped as a massive,
fertile woman holding a sword in one hand for power and a wreath
of flowers in the other for glory. Not yet raised to her pedestal, she
looked out of place" (1:120). By the time of the second inauguration, in the fourth volume, Liberty no longer seems out of place.
Four years before, "The bronze figure of the matron Liberty lay
abandoned on the ground; now she had been lifted to the supreme
height of the Capitol, Walt Whitman writing of it, 'I like to stand
aside and look a long, long while, up at the dome; it comforts me
somehow'" (4:91–92).

The burden of meaning in *The Prairie Years* and *The War Years*
is carried not only by Sandburg's emplotment of the Lincoln story
but also by his management of narrative voice. As a "poetic" biographer, Sandburg largely ignores the convention of the suppression
of his own narrative voice. Far from striving for a neutral, transpar-
ent style, he cultivates a self-consciously poetic style, not only in the
lengthy landscape descriptions of *The Prairie Years* but also in what
he proudly referred to as the "Bach and Sibelius" rhythms of his

"symphonic" finish (1968:373). Sandburg perhaps regarded his self-consciously lyrical prose as employed in the service of his material, bringing out its inherent beauty and drama. Its effect, though, is to keep Sandburg himself constantly before us, along with his subject, and the book has the quality of an immensely extended negotiation between writer and subject, a meditation by Sandburg on Lincoln, in which our attention is on the meditator as often as it is on the object of his meditations. Perhaps the perception that *The Prairie Years* and *The War Years* are "literature" rather than "history" stems, more than anything else, from this foregrounding of the writer's persona and language.

The concern behind Sandburg's meditations and the root of his immensely inflated Lincoln project may perhaps be clarified by placing the book, as discourse, back into its scene of writing, the 1920s and 1930s. Sandburg's *Lincoln* has been usefully historicized against the background of the Great Depression and prewar America in Alfred H. Jones's *Roosevelt's Image Brokers: Poets, Playwrights, and the Use of the Lincoln Symbol* (1974), and Sandburg himself suggests the contemporary implications of his Lincoln studies in a 1935 letter to Franklin D. Roosevelt: "Having written for ten years now on 'Abraham Lincoln: the War Years,' starting this year on the fourth and final volume, I have my eyes and ears in two eras and can not help drawing parallels. One runs to the effect that you are the best light of democracy that has occupied the White House since Lincoln" (1968:318). Writing in an America in economic collapse, with Hitler casting an ever-longer shadow across the world, Sandburg creates a Lincoln who embodies a mystic faith that the American democratic experiment could survive. The impending crisis that darkens the later pages of *The Prairie Years* and the holocaust of *The War Years* are colored by Sandburg's perceptions of 1930s America and his anticipation of world conflict that would test America, as the Civil War had tested it before.

These parallels are also suggested in the passages in which Sandburg directly intrudes into the narrative to comment on its meaning, the running commentary or argument for which Hayden White employs the useful term *diagesis* (1978:4) and which Sandburg called "occasional interpolations of meditations, sometimes musical, having to do with any and all human times" (1968:372). Some of the most interesting of these are meditations on the book itself, metameditations on the problems of writing Lincoln. When, in writing about the Reconstruction constitution of Louisiana, he comments, "Heavy folios of narrative would be required to tell the entire story in all its chaotic and troubled light" (4:79), we are invited also to think of the heavy folios before us with all their own chaotic and troubled lights. More specific is a passage Sandburg quotes from the *New York Herald* on the occasion of Lincoln's death: "A new kind of historian, said the *Herald,* would be required 'to comprehend the genius of a character so externally uncouth, so pathetically simple, so unfathomably penetrating, so irresolute and yet so irresistible, so bizarre, grotesque, droll, wise and perfectly beneficent as the great original thinker and statesman for whose death the whole land, even in the midst of victories unparalleled, is today draped in mourning.'" Wise words, Sandburg thinks, "for any and all who in the future should try to write truly, honestly, decently, adequately, about Abraham Lincoln" (4:369).

Still more to the point is Sandburg's attention to analogues of his own book, pieces of writing that affected the making and the conduct of the disastrous war. He devotes great attention to Lincoln's 1861 Message to Congress in which he attacked the secessionist, educated classes that had engaged in *"an insidious debauching of the public mind"* and goes on to comment:

> Under the political necessities of the hour Lincoln could not have gone so far as to make it clear that in the debates with Douglas he had referred to the Northern public mind's being debauched no less than the Southern, that the masses of people in the North were no more difficult to drug with propaganda than those of the South, and that the North equally with the South had its instruments of rostrum, pulpit, press, for the spreading of the "ingenious sophism" and the dignifying of the "farcical pretense." (1:297)

Throughout the book, Sandburg devotes a great deal of attention to the newspapers and the role they played in shaping public opinion. *The Prairie Years* and *The War Years,* it is clear at least by implication, are an attempt at democratic education; they are intended to inform rather than debauch the public mind, to provide the sort of accurate people's history on which the American dream of popular government depends.

Such a people's history, Sandburg implies, must include both fact and dream: the reality of national failure and the promise of national triumph—"the steel of fact and the fog of dream" (1:8). "America had these lights and contradictions in 1864," Sandburg writes. "Any historian of them in their vast and moving variety needed a gift for showing chaos in the present scene and a weave of paradox leading to the future. A mystic dream of a majestic Republic holding to human freedom and equal opportunity ran parallel to motives of hard cash and pay dirt" (3:615).

The antinomies in these passages—steel of fact and fog of dream, chaos in the present scene and a weave of paradox leading to the future—suggest opposing centrifugal and centripetal impulses in the book, one toward endless proliferation, the other toward control and containment. They thus suggest a third discursive feature of the book, its figuration, or tropological structure. *The Prairie Years* and *The War Years,* which seem produced mainly by accretion, by a piling up of miscellaneous Lincoln material, would seem to be the ultimate metonymic books. Indeed it sometimes seems that anything remotely connected with Lincoln can find a place within its capacious boundaries. A chapter in *The Prairie Years* is devoted to a roll call of Lincoln's law cases in Springfield, many of them commonplace, with no conclusion drawn about Lincoln's approach to the law other than a terminal "Such were a few of the human causes, disputes, and actions in which Lincoln versed himself thoroughly" (2:67). Another merely lists various superstitions and folksayings reported from Kentucky and Indiana that Lincoln might have heard (1:65–70).

Such loose collections of material are examples of a tendency that weakens much of Sandburg's work, as a poet as well as a writer of prose: the tendency to preserve the "natural" form of a piece of material—an anecdote, a fact, a folksaying—rather than give it an artistic form and meaning. Late in his life, Sandburg wrote a poem called "Waiting for the Chariot" in which he asked the question, "Can bare fact make the cloth of a shining poem?" (1970:695), answering it with a barely versified anecdote about the widow of the circuit rider Peter Cartwright. Although the poem is supposed to answer the question affirmatively, the matter is not so simple. The poem demonstrates that "bare fact" can make this sort of poem, one in which unmediated reality is presumed to speak directly to us, much as in a John Cage composition. In the Lincoln biography, as in the poetry, the reader is likely, however, to feel that the material is too often left to speak for itself, that some ineffable meaning is intended to emerge from the raw material on its own.

The centripetal, metonymic structure of *The Prairie Years* and *The War Years* is countered and contained to some degree by descriptions of nature, especially when those descriptions move beyond metonymic figures linked to the central subject of Lincoln only by contiguity and become metaphors, figures linked by figurative similarity. The most important of such natural metaphors in the book is corn, perhaps Sandburg's variation on Whitman's grass, as the homeliest and most democratic of metaphors. Throughout *The Prairie Years* the cycle of the Illinois corn crop becomes a metaphor for the natural rhythms of Lincoln's prairie years and his slow, natural maturation. Chapter 66 is wholly devoted to a description of "the ways of growing corn," linked to the narrative only by a perfunctory reference to Lincoln, "once in late summer" (1:322) passing a field of corn. The stages in the corn season are detailed with loving care, from the spring plowing and planting through the summer maturation to the autumn harvest and the dormancy of winter.

This extraordinary passage is echoed later in Sandburg's description of Lincoln's growth. When he was eleven, Lincoln's "juices and glands began to make a long, tall boy out of him," and people said that "he was shooting up into the air like green corn in the summer of a good corn-year" (1:43). When he works barefooted in the cornfields, his feet are rooted in the earth like the roots of the corn itself:

> In the corn-fields, plowing, hoeing, cutting, and shucking, again his bare feet spoke with the clay of the earth. . . . During six and seven months each year in the twelve fiercest formative years of his life, Abraham Lincoln had the pads of his foot-soles bare against the clay of the earth. It may be the earth told him in her own tough gypsy slang one or two knacks of living worth keeping. To be organic with running wildfire and quiet rain, both of the same moment, is to be the carrier of wave-lines the earth gives up only on hard usage. (1:49)

As Lincoln makes his famous Lost Speech at the first Illinois Republican convention in 1856, which foreshadows his rise to power, "the tiniest sort of corn leaves were coming up in rows in a field near the corner of Eighth and Jackson Streets" (2:30). To skip over many intermediate references, Sandburg recalls the House Divided Speech when Lincoln is elected president and notes that "twice, since he had first so spoken, the corn had grown from seed to the full stalk and been harvested. . . . Winter would come and go before seed corn went into the ground again" (2:373). Metaphorically, the winter of the Civil War does come and go, through the four long volumes of *The War Years,* before, in the April springtime, Lincoln's body comes back to be planted in the Illinois soil, like a primitive corn-god.

This nature-religion imagery may be regarded as corny in more ways than one, but structurally it serves a function beyond the mere deification of Lincoln. Against the "chaos in the present scene," represented by the metonymic accumulation of hard fact, it provides a metaphor for "a weave of paradox leading to the future," grounds for hope that in 1939, as in 1861, the nation might weather a long winter and that eventually the seeds would go in the ground again.

Abraham Lincoln: The Prairie Years and the War Years is, like all Lincoln narratives, a "construct of factual materials shaped and cemented with imagination," and if its factual materials are less reliable than we would wish them to be and if Sandburg's imagination is very much that of the Great Depression and prewar America, we need not conclude that it is merely "myth" and therefore worthless. Sandburg's Lincoln is, of course, not Lincoln, but he is *a* Lincoln, and to recognize the historical situation that shaped this Lincoln is a necessary prelude to interpretation and evaluation.

David Herbert Donald suggested that as *Herndon's Lincoln* slipped further into the past it was being transformed from "history" into "literature." Could the point be generalized into a principle? As historical writing gets older, are we less likely to accept its interpretations as "natural" and thus more likely to see it as artifice? The proposition could also be reversed. Perhaps as "literature" gets older, it turns more and more into "history," an expression not so much of our experience of the world as of the experience of others in other historical situations.

The Lincolns of Illinois writers hover somewhere between literature and history. Probably the least interesting response is to draw the line too rigidly between the categories, to assume that representations of Lincoln are necessarily either "real" or "mythic." Perhaps we should instead delight in a plethora of Lincolns, all more or less "constructs of factual materials shaped and cemented with imagination," some tending to the factual pole, others to the imaginative one, but all making their contribution to our understanding of how we make the events of the past do the cultural work of today.

3

Writing Chicago

In 1986, Studs Terkel, the Chicago oral historian and broadcaster, published a short book called *Chicago,* a free-form monologue incorporating personal reminiscences, wry anecdotes from Chicago's history, snippets from interviews in Terkel's previous books, and descriptions of the city. One of Terkel's reviewers (Harold Henderson) sharply questioned the accuracy of the book; Terkel was writing, he said, about "a city that is no longer there" (11). This seemed a curious charge to make against a book that was frankly nostalgic, oriented to both a personal past and a municipal one. Even more problematical was the reviewer's assumption that Terkel was writing about an objective reality to which the reviewer had direct access and against which he could measure the accuracy of Terkel's book. This assumption apparently seemed so self-evident to the reviewer that he did not bother to define what the real Chicago was that Terkel had failed to describe. It was not a matter of the accuracy of Terkel's facts—the reviewer did not question them—but rather his tone: his nostalgia, his idealization of the working class, and his attitude of bemusement rather than anger over Chicago's tradition of corruption. "Strange," the reviewer commented. "He admires the deal-makers—and hates the deals!" (11).

At the heart of this little debate (a one-sided one, to be sure) was an implicit disagreement over what was at issue. What is the "Chicago" over which Terkel and his reviewer disagreed? Is it the concrete city or a conceptual construction? The reviewer assumed that it was the actual city, but he objected not to factual inaccuracies but to the way that Terkel conceptualized the city. The disagreement, in other words, was not over what Chicago is but rather over how it should be represented, a disagreement over discourse.

It was not a new disagreement. Chicago's mushroom growth in the late nineteenth century to prominence among the world's cities was paralleled by a second, shadow growth of Chicago discourse, an explosion of describing, fictionalizing, and mythologizing without parallel among American cities. "Since stories attract stories and fictions generate counter-fictions," the Chicago novelist Richard Stern has recently written, "this most fictionalized of American cities grows ever thicker with its selves, so much so that between the fictions and the actualities, there is hardly room for a shadow" (29). "Chicago," he says, "is as much a verbal as a stone and metal construction" (23).

The writing of Chicago, like the writing of the prairie and of Lincoln, has been, in a sense, an attempt to make something out of nothing. Like the prairie and Lincoln, Chicago presented to its interpreters something seemingly new in history, a novelty perceived as a lack. As the flat, empty prairie lacked the features of a recognizably habitable landscape and as Lincoln lacked the traditional preparation and qualifications for leadership, so Chicago, raw, corrupt, and wholly commercialized, seemed to lack the necessary prerequisites for culture. The process of interpretation has recurringly been a process of naturalization, of relating aspects of the city to recognizable traditions while allowing for its innovations, a complex interweaving of old and new.

Canonical Chicago

The history of Chicago literature, as it has been written and rewritten, has gradually taken on a certain shape, a shape illustrated by, for example, Henry Claridge's recent "Chicago: 'The Classical Center of American Materialism'" (1988). Claridge begins with Henry Adams's interpretation of the 1893 Chicago World's Fair. Adams found that the fair raised the question of whether Chicago could be said to have a culture and, if so, whether its citizens took any interest in it, as well as the more general one of whether "materialism, or commercial life, and artistic culture are mutually exclusive conditions" (89). Claridge sees these questions as underlying much of Chicago literature, from Henry Blake Fuller to Saul Bellow.

Chicago literature, then, begins in the 1890s, in Fuller's novels. This was the first budding of the "Chicago Renaissance," which blossomed in the years after 1900, when "a wave of writers, some major, some minor, converged on Chicago and, effectively, created a literary culture for the city: Sherwood Anderson from Clyde, Ohio; Floyd Dell from Davenport, Iowa; Theodore Dreiser from Terre Haute, Indiana; Ben Hecht from New York; Robert Herrick from Boston; Vachel Lindsay from Springfield, Illinois; Edgar Lee Masters from Lewistown, Illinois; Carl Sandburg from Galesburg, Illinois" (Claridge 96). These writers, we are told, drew together two Chicago traditions: urban reform (exemplified by Jane Addams, John Dewey, and Thorstein Veblen) and the demand for greater personal and artistic freedom, generally called "the revolt against the village." The achievement of the Chicago Renaissance writers was, according to Claridge, a double victory: "the victory of the urban over the rural and the victory of unbridled realism over cautious gentility in the arts" (99).

The four most important Chicago writers since the end of the Chicago Renaissance in the early 1920s, according to Claridge (and the only ones he names), are James T. Farrell, Nelson Algren, Richard Wright, and Saul Bellow. None of the four has been much influenced by modernism; all four remain firmly within the realistic tradition, which has been the "dominant mode of writing about the city" (100). In Farrell's *Studs Lonigan* (1932–35), "the city is treated simply as brutalizing and degrading" (100). Nelson Algren and Richard Wright discard Farrell's documentary realism in favor of "a kind of atmospheric realism" in which "the world of the city becomes increasingly nightmarish and impalpable" (101). Wright's Chicago is a "world circumscribed by poverty and brutality," while Algren's Near North Side is "brutalized in much the same way as Wright's South Side" (101). Bellow's response to Chicago, though "more metonymic than realistic," is "largely negative and pessimistic"; he "disabuses those who think that Chicago culture is anything more than a pretense, and the new city that has grown up around the old is, for him, simply 'proud, synthetic Chicago'" (103).

Claridge's essay is a skillful restatement of the received account of Chicago writing, and certainly one does not expect much depth or detail in an eight-thousand-word essay. But its very brevity makes the traditional narrativization of Chicago literary history stand out with a skeletal clarity and points up its limitations. Thirteen writers appear by name. All are male, and all but Richard Wright are white. The approach is resolutely belletristic, weighted heavily toward novels. Such figures as Jane Addams and Thorstein Veblen appear as sources for writers but not as writers themselves, though such books as *Twenty Years at Hull-House* and *The Theory of the Leisure Class* are, by most criteria, of more literary interest than, say, Frank Norris's *The Pit*. Vachel Lindsay, Edgar Lee Masters, and Carl Sandburg are invoked, but only as names; one would not know from Claridge's account that they wrote poems. Furthermore, Claridge makes his subject more manageable by lopping off both ends of his chronology. The first three-quarters of a century of Chicago history, by his account, produced no literature, and the past forty years are represented only by the novels of Saul Bellow.

Claridge, of course, did not invent this dubious narrative; it has prevailed for many years as the dominant account of the literary history of Chicago. Fortunately, it has been increasingly eroded over the past few years by a number of critical reconsiderations. Ross Miller, for example, in *American Apocalypse: The Great Fire and the Myth of Chicago,* has exploded the notion that Chicago literature began with Henry Blake Fuller by reading closely and sympathetically the literature of the 1871 Chicago Fire; Kenny J. Williams's *Prairie Voices* stops at 1893 rather than beginning there. Sidney Bremer, in several essays, has demonstrated that the novels of Edith Wyatt, Elia Peattie, Clara Burnham, Susan Glaspell, Clara Laughlin, Alice Gerstenberg, and Willa Cather constitute a turn-of-the-century countertradition of Chicago women's writing that presented "alternative urban visions." She finds that this alternative tradition presented Chicago not as mechanical, inhuman, and brutal but as "informed by communal concerns, interfused with organic nature, and enmeshed in familial continuities" (1984:210). Carl S. Smith, in *Chicago and the American Literary Imagination, 1880–1920,* has reread the fiction of turn-of-the-century Chicago and shown that it constructs a far richer imaginative Chicago than "the stupendous piece of blasphemy against nature" of Robert Herrick's famous 1898 description (103–4). Such readers of "social texts," rather than narrowly literary ones, as Kenny J. Williams, Hugh D. Duncan, and

Allen F. Davis have incorporated such works as William T. Stead's *If Christ Came to Chicago!* (1894), Louis Sullivan's *Autobiography of an Idea* (1924), and Jane Addams's *Twenty Years at Hull-House* (1910) into the literature of Chicago. Ann Douglas and Lewis F. Fried have, in different ways, made it impossible to see James T. Farrell's Chicago as "simply" brutalizing and degrading. A number of writers have called attention to the richness and diversity of contemporary Chicago writing, which is far more likely to present the city as an infinitely rich environment of cultural diversity than as a jungle or a pit.

It is this last point I would like to develop here, in a brief survey of how Chicago has been constructed in a sampling of recent Chicago writing, beginning with two books linked in a curious dialogic relationship: Nelson Algren's *Chicago: City on the Make* (1951) and Studs Terkel's *Chicago* (1986). I will then turn to three short-story collections and a novel: Cyrus Colter's *Beach Umbrella* (1970), Maxine Chernoff's *Bop* (1986), Stuart Dybek's *Coast of Chicago* (1990), and Paul Hoover's fine 1988 novel *Saigon, Illinois*. I will conclude with an extended look at the Chicago of Saul Bellow's fiction. This is a tiny sampling of contemporary Chicago writing, but even within its narrow limits Chicago is represented in a wide variety of ways, from the dizzyingly complex variety of Colter's microcosmic Black Chicago and the mundane reality, likely at any moment to turn surreal, of Chernoff's city, to Dybek's nostalgically romantic ethnic Chicago, Hoover's Chicago of the sixties, charged by the consciousness of the narrator with the conflicts of a war half a world away, and Saul Bellow's ambiguous Chicago, which preserves, in some ways, the traditional myth of a brutalizing city, while countering it with the perspective of European culture. Different as these Chicagos are from one another, they are all recentered Chicagos; they have escaped the myth, expressed by Claridge, of a brutal Chicago wholly given over to male Oedipal conflict.

The Chicagos of Nelson Algren and Studs Terkel

The transition from the realistic-naturalistic tradition in Chicago writing to a more open and pluralistic one can be seen quite clearly in two closely linked books: Nelson Algren's *Chicago: City on the Make* and Studs Terkel's *Chicago*. Terkel calls *Chicago* merely "a long epilogue" to Algren's (131). Algren's book already had a complex history. He expanded the seven sections of the original edition of 1951 with a lengthy section called "The People of These Parts" for a second edition in 1961. In it, he reviewed the hostile reception the first edition received in Chicago and defended his characterization of the city. When a third edition appeared in 1983, it had picked up an introduction by Terkel that not only praised the original version but commented favorably on Algren's 1961 commentary as well. This introduction, in turn, was reprinted as an afterword to Terkel's own 1986 "prose poem," which carries the dedication "This is for Nelson Algren." Thus the two books in their various versions—1951, 1961, 1983, and 1986—can be read as a single developing discourse that periodically looks back and comments on itself.

Chicago: City on the Make is virtually a valedictory statement of the traditional mythology, a catalogue of stock motifs. Algren divides the city into opposites: it "keeps two faces, one for winners and one for losers; one for hustlers and one for squares. . . . One for poets and one for promoters. One for the good boy and one for the bad," and so forth (23–24). He sees it as an artificial construction barely holding at bay a nature constantly reasserting itself: "Littered with tin cans and dark with smoldering rubble, an Indian wind yet finds, between the shadowed canyons of The Loop, patches of prairie to touch and pass" (76). When night falls, the city regresses to barbarism as "the jungle hiders" come forth under the El (59). It is indisputably real: "Like loving a woman with a broken nose, you may well find lovelier lovelies. But never a lovely so real" (23). Despite the analogy of the woman with a broken nose, Chicago is a male city, the field of male competition in crime, politics, and sport (with the three overlapping considerably).

Overlaying these various oppositions is one that incorporates them all: hustlers and squares. The original settlers of Chicago had "hustler's blood" (11); they "hustled by night and they hustled by day" (12). Algren's favorite image for Chicago life is the rigged ball game. Much of the third section of the book is devoted to a lengthy anecdote about how Algren as a young boy told his friends that Swede Risberg, shortstop for the Chicago White Sox, whom Algren saw play, was his "fayvrut player" (34). The year is 1919, and Risberg and his team are revealed within a few months to have thrown the World Series. The youthful Algren has to defend himself against his friends' ridicule that he had watched Risberg play and didn't realize he was crooked. The point of this little maturational story seems to be that to grow up is to realize that everyone is a hustler. "I guess that was one way of learning what Hustlertown, sooner or later, teaches all its sandlot sprouts. 'Everybody's out for The Buck. Even big-leaguers.' Even Swede Risberg" (39).

Algren's figure for Chicago is a childhood friend's Uncle Johnson, a pathetic drunk who is lured into a hopeless fight every Saturday night outside his favorite saloon. Some young hoodlum always waits until Johnson is drunk and then challenges him to a fight: "Uncle had never learned to fall down. He'd reel, lurch, bleed, bellow and bawl until the bartender would break the thing up at last, wiping Uncle's ashen face with a bar towel in the arc-lamp's ashen light. . . . Uncle had some such spiritual triumph every Saturday night" (32–33). Chicago, Algren tells us, is a "Johnson of a city" (49), perhaps in ironic commentary on Sandburg's "tall bold slugger." The ignorant fighter who has "never lost a battle" has become a punchy drunk who never wins one.

Uncle Johnson's fights are another version of the rigged ball game; he doesn't know that he's being set up. The young punk is the hustler, Uncle Johnson the square. But here, and in the book as a whole, Algren's own allegiances are ambiguous. Johnson's own nephew roots for the punk: "Finish the clown off" (32). Algren is ostensibly on the side of Johnson—and of all the derelicts, prostitutes, and "working stiffs" he stands in for—but his sympathy is often tinged with contempt, and we sense an admiration, somewhat repressed, for the wised-up hustler. Even the vote-buying Hinky Dink Kenna comes in for his share of praise: "Yet in standardizing the price of the vote The Hink did more to keep the city running one bitter winter than did all the balmy summers of Moody's evangelism. . . . It always takes somebody like The Hink, in whom avarice and generosity mingled like the hot rum and the cold water in his own Tom-and-Jerries, to run a city wherein warmth of heart and a freezing greed beat, like the blood and the breath, as one" (21).

Algren's divided allegiances are also apparent in his treating tough, urban material in a lush style that Saul Maloff accurately described as "overblown, elegaic, tremulous, quivering, cadenced or wistful celebratory nostalgia that used to be called prose poetry" (23). Here, for example, is the ending of the book:

The Pottawattomies were much too square. They left nothing behind
but their dirty river.
While we shall leave, for remembrance, one rusty iron heart.
The city's rusty heart, that holds both the hustler and the square.
Takes them both and holds them there.
For keeps and a single day. (77)

For all the moral fervor of Algren's defense of his Uncle Johnson squares, the effect of such writing as this is to transcend the
social and political judgments that Algren's material invites. Tacitly
contemptuous of his sentimentalized squares, tacitly respectful of
his voracious hustlers, Algren finally awards them equal place in the
city's imaginary "rusty heart."

There is something in Algren's attitude of what Pat Colander, in
*Hugh Hefner's First Funeral and Other True Tales of Love and Death
in Chicago,* has called the "Second City voodoo": the stance that if
one can't be best, the next best thing is to be the worst. "Maybe our
forefathers," Colander writes, "knew that striving for real achievement was too painful and lengthy a process. Better to grab the berth
no one wanted: the most unholy climate, the rankest charlatans, the
greediest thieves, the most vicious gangsters, most blatant liars, and
most amateurish culture" (3).

Terkel's *Chicago* both incorporates the Second City voodoo and
comically dismantles it. It is more than simple homage to Algren; it
reveals not just the influence of Algren but also what Harold Bloom
calls the "anxiety of influence." Terkel misreads Algren, and, in the
process of rewriting him, produces his own original vision of Chicago. Terkel reads Algren as a "street-corner comic. . . . the funniest
man around" (132). "Algren," he writes, "may be remembered as
something of a Gavroche, the gamin who saw it all, with an admix-
ture of innocence and wisdom. And indignation" (133). It is Terkel,
not Algren, that Terkel is describing. There is a certain rather bitter,
ironic comedy occasionally in Algren, along with, more frequently,
a humorlessness that makes possible his romantic stylistic excesses.
But it is Terkel who writes with a pervasive genial humor that mixes
"innocence and wisdom."

Chicago incorporates all the old ways of representing Chicago,
but they are handled with comic irony. Chicago is Hustlertown?
In his opening lines, Terkel acknowledges the question and turns it

into comedy by peopling Abraham Lincoln's nominating convention with modern Chicagoans: "When Abe Lincoln came out of the wilderness and loped off with the Republican nomination on that memorable May day, 1860, the Wigwam had been resonant with whispers. Behind cupped hands, lips imperceptibly moved: We just give Si Cameron Treasury, they give us Pennsylvania, Abe's got it wrapped up. OK wit'chu? A wink. A nod. Done. It was a classic deal, Chicago style" (3). If Algren's exemplary figure for Chicago is drunken Uncle Johnson, beaten but unable to fall down, Terkel's is Jessie Binford, Jane Addams's associate and leader of the 1962 fight to save Hull-House from being razed to make room for the new Chicago campus of the University of Illinois. Binford's story and that of her much younger fellow protester Florence Scala run through the book like a connecting thread. Superficially, their story is one of defeat: "They lost, of course. Betrayed right down the line. By our city's Most Respectable" (8). But Terkel's emphasis is not on winning or losing but on a spirit of cooperation and community: the fact that in their common fight, Binford and Scala "came to know one another and value one another, as they clasped hands to save these streets" (8). The Hull-House buildings may fall to the wrecking ball, but the spirit of Jane Addams is passed as a legacy from her generation to the present one in the figures of Binford and Scala.

Algren's heroes are lonely male individualists locked in power struggles, whether as artists or gangsters: "It used to be a writer's town and it's always been a fighter's town. . . . Whether the power is in a .38, a typewriter ribbon or a pair of six-ouncers, the place has grown great on bone-deep grudges to settle" (62). Terkel's heroes are people who, sometimes in small ways, humanize the city: the mural artists of the thirties and their contemporary successors, the street wall artists; a widow named Elizabeth Chapin who takes lonely shut-ins to the Art Institute and Lincoln Park; Barry Byrne, once an apprentice to Frank Lloyd Wright, who dreams of building a city that would be "a place to *live*" (95); and all the people of Chicago in 1967, when a paralyzing snow turned the city temporarily into a friendly community. (Characteristically, Terkel deflates his own perhaps too earnest interpretation by citing Mike Royko's: the real significance of the snow was that "it gave people a chance to stay downtown overnight and get drunk" [105].)

Alternative Chicagos

The dismantling of the naturalistic myth of Chicago illustrated by Terkel's *Chicago* has also been taking place among fiction
writers, including Cyrus Colter, Maxine Chernoff, Stuart Dybek,
and Paul Hoover. A special, book-length issue of *TriQuarterly* magazine named *Chicago* (1984) contained a roundtable discussion of
"The Writer in Chicago," by Chernoff, Colter, Dybek, Reginald
Gibbons, and Fred Shafer. In the course of the discussion, Colter
defined his goal as a writer in these terms:

> I do, I think, what most black writers have so far pretty much not chosen
> to do—I write about *all kinds* of blacks. From the low to the high and
> back again. There is a great gamut here, a tremendously wide range—
> contrary to what many people, including apparently some black writers,
> think. So while I write perhaps predominantly of the black underclass—
> for that's where much of heartbreak and anguish is to be found—I also
> explore, with sympathy, I hope, the black middle class, and the intellec-
> tuals, even the burgeoning black upper class. (Gibbons and Shafer 327)

When Colter's first book (and only short-story collection) *The
Beach Umbrella* was published in 1970, it struck a startlingly new
note in Chicago fiction. In the long tradition of distinguished Black
Chicago writing, no one had ever presented the Black community
so comprehensively as Colter did. In the fourteen deceptively simple
and elegantly crafted stories of the collection, Colter ranges over the
South Side, the Southwest Side, and isolated locations elsewhere to
build up a systematic, inclusive picture of a city and a people.

The project is reminiscent of Joyce's *Dubliners*, and Colter acknowledges that he began the stories of the collection after he "had
read *Dubliners* a couple of times" (Gibbons and Shafer 338). Like
Dubliners, The Beach Umbrella has an overall design, rather than
being a random collection, and like Joyce, Colter presents his characters not in isolation but as the products of an especially deadening
urban milieu. Most important, as in Joyce, the emphasis is not so
much on external, social oppression as on its internalized version, a
kind of paralysis that repeatedly results in self-defeat.

The powerful title story, which ends the collection, in some ways
demonstrates the recurring action of many of these stories. Elijah,
a forty-one-year-old underpaid warehouse clerk, escapes every Sunday from his discontented wife and two children to the Thirty-first

Street beach, where he broods on his woes and envies the seemingly carefree parties under their brightly colored beach umbrellas. He eventually decides to buy a beach umbrella himself, as if this would solve his problems. He buys it, with fifteen dollars borrowed from his twelve-year-old son—his wife Myrtle handles his own money— and spends a nervously happy afternoon at the beach, managing to attract a few strays to his beach umbrella and his lemonade jug. But at the end of the day, his new friends abandon him, and he is left alone with the now useless umbrella and no way to pay the fifteen dollars back to his son.

Elijah is encaged at the beginning of the story; he makes an attempt at escape, but the door of his cage slams even more firmly shut at the end. But what is the cage? Certainly Elijah is a victim of poverty, ignorance, and racism. His job does not pay enough for his family to live on, even minimally, and the only alternative seems to be a grueling, dangerous job at Youngstown Sheet and Tube, "pouring that white-hot ore" (203). He also feels that he is under the thumb of his domineering wife. Her worry about school starting and the need for clothes and books seems reasonable, however, and even Elijah is forced to admit that "she never griped about anything for herself; only for the family and kids" (203). Moreover, Elijah's real objection to a steel mill job is not that it is dangerous but that it is "undignified"; he likes his "whitecollar" job, the tie he wears to work, and the ballpoint pen and clipboard he carries with him on his inventory rounds (203).

Elijah is primarily the victim of his own inadequacy. He cuts a ludicrous figure at the beach, with his skinny, bowed legs and his jerky, spidery walk. He humiliates himself by trying to ingratiate himself with strangers and suffers insults and rebuffs humbly. He is slavishly afraid of authority; when one of his beach-umbrella "friends" pours gin in his lemonade, Elijah shakes his head and whispers, "You ain't supposed to drink on the beach, y'know" (215). Most of all, Elijah is the victim of his own poverty of imagination, pinning his hopes for happiness on the tragicomically inadequate beach umbrella and unable to foresee the consequences of his impulsive stab at empowerment.

The pattern of a thrust toward freedom and the thwarting of that thrust is anticipated many times in the earlier stories of the collection. Essie, in "The Rescue," resolves to escape from her brutal, drunken boyfriend by moving to Cleveland. But when she cannot persuade her younger sister, for whom she feels responsible, to go with her, she returns to her boyfriend and screams at him, "*You rotten, no-good, black son-of-a-bitch,* you! *I'll* marry you!" (54). The well-to-do Laura, in "The Lookout," whose emotional investment is solely in her husband's financial success, realizes that he is slipping behind and finds herself in her expensive car sitting outside a wealthy friend's house and watching guests arrive at a party to which she is not invited. Amos, in "An Overnight Trip," makes an attempt at happiness by marrying a loving young wife but realizes that he is losing her through his own anxious inadequacy.

Colter arranges his stories dialectically, so that stories presenting the sharpest contrasts often appear next to one another. The opening story, "A Man in the House," a story of youth (in which seventeen-year-old Verna, visiting her uncle and aunt from Memphis, realizes that she is in danger of becoming sexually involved with her handsome uncle but decides to stay anyway) is followed by "A Chance Meeting," a story of old age (in which Ford, an elderly bachelor music-lover and former servant of the late Mrs. Cate, whom he idealized, learns that Mrs. Cate had a lover). A story of the impoverished, drug-ridden underclass like "Mary's Convert" is followed by "Black for Dinner," set in the "posh Hyde Park–Kenwood black community." A story of female experience, "A Gift" (in which the dying Cora tries to arrange for another wife for her husband after her death), is followed by a story of male experience, "The Beach Umbrella."

The stories in *The Beach Umbrella* are studies, often ironic or even comic ones, in the psychology of a long-oppressed group: the strained relations between strong women and weak men, the yearning for escape from oppressive conditions, the prices paid in the battle for success against overwhelming odds. They are also stories of place; the characters in *The Beach Umbrella* are as intertwined with the city they live in as the characters in *Dubliners* are. In the *TriQuarterly* interview, Colter was asked about the function of place in his work. He replied that he chose Chicago as a setting for the same reason that he chose Black characters: because he knew it best. But he went on to say that, as he wrote, the Chicago setting became more and more important in his characters' lives (Gibbons and Shafer 325–26).

Certainly the stories convey a strong sense of the Black areas of Chicago. Settings are quite specific, and the characters' movements are plotted so precisely that they can be followed on a map. The result is a rich representation of both Chicago and its Black inhabitants. It is an environment sometimes harsh and brutal but just as often warm and hospitable, a complex representation as varied as the people who inhabit it.

Colter's stories often seem to be responses to earlier Chicago fiction, the short stories of James T. Farrell perhaps. It is almost as if he were going over the same material but recentering the narratives in the consciousnesses of the Black figures who slip quietly across the backgrounds of Farrell's fictional stages, as vaguely threatening Others to his Irish-American characters. (Farrell himself occasionally recentered his stories in this way.)

The stories of Maxine Chernoff often seem to be engaged in the same sort of intertextuality. In the title story of her 1986 collection *Bop,* for example, Oleg Lum, a Russian immigrant in Chicago, finds an apparently abandoned baby on the beach, who replies, when Oleg asks his name, merely "Bop." Not wanting to entrust him to the police, he takes him home and then, the next day, to the home of Claire, an American divorcée whom he has met through her ten-year-old daughter, Carrie. Claire has had a hysterectomy, and Oleg briefly fantasizes that she might marry him, keep Bop, and together form a perfect American family: "Suppose she suggested marriage on the spot, Oleg Lum the father of little Bop, she the mother, Carrie the big sister, a home on a quiet street, maybe a dog, lots of American television to cool his rapid-fire brain" (26). But of course Claire sensibly insists that they turn Bop over to the police, and the fantasy is punctured. Later Oleg sadly writes another of his letters, never printed, to the "Personal View" column of the newspaper:

Dear Personal View:
    Everything in America gets lost, sometimes stolen. I lose my umbrella on el train. It is never returned. Meanwhile, baby is left on beach to weather, danger, criminals, drug takers, God knows. Parents come to police. Say they are sorry, so baby is returned. Why in America is easier to find lost baby than umbrella costing nine dollars? But I worry most for sandy American baby who is found on beach like walking rubbish heap called Bop. He is dirty, hungry little immigrant. I give him new life visa, which police revoke. (28)

"Bop" is a rewriting of perhaps the oldest and most durable Chicago plot: the immigrant adrift in the chaotic impersonality of the city, the plot of *Sister Carrie, The Jungle,* and *Native Son,* for example. Here the immigrant is not brutalized and defeated, however. Oleg may feel at the end of the story that, like Bop, his "new life visa" has been revoked by the police, but along the way he has encountered warmth and kindness in his researches into American life, which have led him to fill fourteen scrapbooks with trivia and to fill up his apartment with American kitsch. He has also formed a family of sorts. It may not be the television American family he imagines. Claire's apartment is bare and sterile: "No decorations had been rehung where picture hooks and curtain rods waited. It looked as if a civilization had perished there" (21). As for Claire herself: "She wore furry slippers, blue jeans, a sweat shirt that said SPEED WAGON, and no make-up. Her hair wasn't combed but stuck over one ear as if it had been glued there. Her eyes looked dried up, like African drinking holes" (19). (Later, when they go out, she dresses "as an Indian princess" [22].) But before they turn Bop over to the police, they sit and watch him for an hour: "They sat hand in hand for an hour, Oleg enjoying the most mundane fantasy. They were at an American pediatrician's, taking their child for a checkup. She was the bride he'd met in college, and she still wore her modest wedding ring, though he'd have liked to have been more extravagant. She didn't have to talk, his wife of many years, just sit and admire their little son" (28). Bop is gone, but Claire is still there, and whether she and Oleg ultimately form a permanent family or not, they have created, at least briefly, a home.

Chernoff's Chicago is inviting not only because of the warmth of people like Oleg and Claire but also because of its wealth of unexpected incongruities. Chernoff has discussed her interest in the bizarre aspects of everyday life:

My first story that had any success with publication in terms of a bigger audience was in *Chicago* magazine and that was a story about Sundays with my family and strange things we encountered. Place became the subject of that story. It dealt with drives past the Cracker Jack factory where they had a big surreal pre-Claes-Oldenberg Cracker Jack box on the lawn. . . . Once we saw a man sitting on a bench stark naked. And I realized that the possibilities for strangeness that I wanted in my fabulist early period were also very much of my place. And that's how I started using more of Chicago. (Gibbons and Shafer, 326)

Much of the gentle comedy of "Bop" comes from Chernoff's use of such strangeness. The apartment above Oleg's is occupied by a pair of mimes: "How could two men practicing the art of silence make so much noise? Was it the rope pull or the human washing machine they were doing? Were they sizzling down to the floor like angry bacon, or were they sentimental clowns on an invisible tight-rope? He hated what they did. It reminded him of loneliness, of which he already had enough evidence" (14). Oleg's noisy mimes do not find their way into the story merely for their strangeness—they obviously serve character—but an urban world that can offer such unexpected delights is far removed from the jungles and pits of canonized Chicago fiction.

The major sources of strangeness in Chernoff's stories are their people. In a significant number of her stories, a comparatively conventional person meets a person who is "strange" in some way, and the story explores the significance of the relationship. "That Summer" illustrates the pattern very well. Amy, an art student, falls in love with Raymond: "That summer there was Raymond, who prided himself on living through the darkest hours in his own history. Raymond of private schools for disturbed adolescents, of washroom wastebasket fires. Raymond of the insect eyes that never closed, who loved to dance and call celebrities by their first names" (40). Amy, though quiet, introspective, and apparently very different from the flamboyant Raymond, has been something of a "disturbed adolescent" herself. Her mother, "a career woman before the fashion" (41), has been gone during most of Amy's childhood, and her father has also withdrawn into his work.

Raymond drowns in Lake Michigan during a picnic, and the story explores, largely in retrospect, their relationship. Amy realizes that the relationship is partially compensatory, a redoing of her own past: "She realized that she mothered him in contrast to her own mother's lack of involvement, and usually Raymond didn't object" (43). She identifies with Raymond and his unhappy childhood, while at the same time she makes him into her opposite; his comic obscenity makes her think that he was "the lewdest man she'd ever dated . . . Amy's own worst idea of men, blended with the suspicion of his innocence" (41). Amy's father tells Raymond, "We think you're very liberating for Amy" (46), and Amy herself thinks, "He was Amy's way of releasing herself, being real" (45). Amy had designed fabric prints before Raymond's death, "swirling colors, holiday reds and greens, cool blues melting into gray, swimming colors, some dangerous, so light as a glance" (45), but in the autumn after his death, her senior project is a design "so subtle it depended on texture, not color" (48). Her professor tells her that she has matured. Chernoff wisely does not privilege any one dimension of Amy's complex relationship with Raymond. When Amy was eight, she had terrible, homicidal dreams about her mother: "'Because you hate her for leaving you so often,' a therapist once told her. 'Because people die and children are left motherless,' she countered in her clear, eight-year-old voice" (42). Raymond, his death, and her grief are finally as simple and as mysterious as that.

The pairing of a conventional person and an eccentric is repeated, with a great range of meanings, in the contrasts between Susan and her childhood playmate Lacey Davis, who has his leg shot off by his male lover in "Phantom Pleasure," between the elderly Arthur Degan and his drug-dealing grandson in "Degan Dying," and between the American narrator and her unstable refugee friend Mariel in "The Hills of Andorra." Even the relationship between Oleg Lum and Claire in "Bop" follows this pattern, this time from the viewpoint of the eccentric outsider.

In the *TriQuarterly* roundtable, Chernoff was asked about her relationship to the Chicago literary tradition represented by Nelson Algren and James T. Farrell. Chernoff replied, "I don't think that either Algren or Farrell would be choices or role models for a woman writer growing up in Chicago. Many of the writers you think of as the Chicago writers are the brawling, barroom kind of writers that might portray a man's point of view. . . . The male tradition seems to me, in my own writing, as distant as what Carl Sandburg did in poetry, say. I would never attempt to do it now or want to follow it" (Gibbons and Shafer 333). Maxine Chernoff's Chicago is, indeed, remote from Algren's and Farrell's desperate fields of male competition. It is an open network of encounters that celebrate difference, possibility, and surprise.

In Stuart Dybek's story "Blight," in his collection *The Coast of Chicago* (1990), one of David's (the narrator's) neighborhood friends,

Joey "Deejo" DeCampo, is trying to write the Great American Novel. It is named *Blight,* and its first sentence is "The dawn rises like sick old men playing on the rooftops in their underwear." The second sentence is twenty pages long and has nothing to do with the old men on the rooftops in their underwear; it describes "an epic battle between a spider and a caterpillar." David comments, "It wasn't Deejo's digressing that bothered us. That was how we all told stories" (51).

The publisher's blurb on the dust jacket of *The Coast of Chicago* tells us that "Dybek draws on the Chicago tradition of Sandberg, Algren, and Bellow, but he also displays a lyrical associative talent that calls to mind Kafka or Calvino." Fortunately, this is wrong (and not just in the spelling of "Sandburg"). Dybek does not write like Sandburg, Kafka, or the like; he writes like Deejo DeCampo.

Dybek, like Deejo, is writing a piece of fiction named "Blight." David the narrator is remembering his adolescence in the 1950s, when his neighborhood on the Southwest Side around Twenty-second Street was designated by the city as an Official Blight Area. His narrative, like Deejo's, seems to have no structure. Characters are introduced: David's friends Ziggy Zilensky, who starts seeing famous people after being hit on the head with a bat and who eventually hitchhikes to Gethsemane, Kentucky, to join the Trappists; Stanley "Pepper" Rosado, who has internalized the conflicts of his parents' Polish-Mexican marriage and finally flees to the Marine Corps; and Deejo himself, poet and novelist, who would write songs if he could think of a bridge and if he could spell. Things happen in "Blight": the friends start a band named the Blighters, Pepper pursues an unrequited passion for Linda Molina, the friends venture out in a worn-out '53 Chevy, the White Sox win the pennant. But there is no plot in the ordinary sense. David uses a catchphrase from his friends to call attention to his own rambling. The friends take a wry, shamefaced pride in living in an Official Blight Area. When they ride the subway north to the Oak Street beach, they cry "North to freedom!" and on the way back someone always says, "Back to blight." Now, when David's memories stray too far off his ostensible subject, he calls them back to order by writing, "Back to blight." The story has no center to return to, however, not even "blight"; it is all digression, like Deejo's surprising narrative.

The same thing might be said of *The Coast of Chicago* as a whole; it is a collection of narrative fragments that cohere not through linear logic but through the associational logic of dream and memory. The epigraph, from Antonio Machado, accurately describes the collection: "*De toda la memoria, solo vale el don preclare de evocare los suenos.* (Out of the whole of memory, there's one thing worthwhile: the great gift of calling back dreams.)"

The Coast of Chicago consists of seven stories, each preceded by an "outtake," a short sketch, from half a page to three or four pages, that records a brief memory. The relationships between these outtakes and the stories they introduce are varied and oblique. The simplest, perhaps, is one called "Outtakes" (72–73), a magical sketch about a movie usher who can fly, which introduces "Bijou," an account of a surrealistic film. "The Woman Who Fainted" (119–22) is a boyhood memory of an attractive woman who often fainted during Sunday mass. It introduces "Hot Ice," a marvellously complex story that deals with, among other things, folk Catholicism. "Blight" is introduced by "Bottle Caps," a sketch about a boy who uses bottle caps for tombstones in his insect graveyard, anticipating the longer story's theme of environmental meagerness.

The same dust jacket that compares Dybek with Sandburg, Algren, and Bellow compares *The Coast of Chicago* with "Joyce's *Dubliners,* Anderson's *Winesburg, Ohio,* and Babel's *Tales of Odessa.*" The comparison is valid insofar as *The Coast of Chicago* is a collection of linked stories with a common urban setting, but *The Coast of Chicago* is not otherwise much like *Dubliners,* not nearly so much like it as Colter's *Beach Umbrella* is. Joyce is not much interested in dream and memory in the sense of Dybek's epigraph; the first three stories in *Dubliners* are boyhood memories, but they are cool and ironic in tone, and thereafter the stories are set in the present and are even more detached.

The larger theme that runs through Dybek's stories is the nature of culture. The wonderful story "Chopin in Winter" exemplifies the theme. The story begins, "The winter Dzia-Dzia came to live with us in Mrs. Kubiac's building on Eighteenth Street was the winter that Mrs. Kubiac's daughter, Marcy, came home pregnant from college in New York" (7), and the story traces out the counterpointed stories of Dzia-Dzia and Marcy. Dzia-Dzia is Michael's (the narrator's) grandfather, who after a lifetime of wandering, sits silently in his daughter's kitchen soaking his feet in a bright pink medicinal bath. Marcy is a pianist and thunderously plays Chopin in the apartment upstairs after supper every night. Listening to the music, Dzia-Dzia, who has never betrayed an interest in any music but the "Frankie Yankovitch Polka Hour," breaks his silence, teaches Michael the names of all the Chopin pieces, and mimes Marcy's playing on the kitchen table. As Marcy's pregnancy advances, she plays less often, and Dzia-Dzia lapses back into silence and footbaths. As winter ends, Dzia-Dzia goes back on the road, and Marcy disappears, to surface months later, living on the South Side with a Black man, the father of her child.

High and low cultures are juxtaposed in Marcy's Chopin upstairs and Dzia-Dzia's Frankie Yankovitch downstairs (both, of course, Polish). The mix is complicated by the Black boogie-woogie that Marcy occasionally plays and that tells the erratically perceptive Dzia-Dzia that "she's in love with a colored man" (14). The spirit of tolerance prevails in Michael's household. His mother hates bigotry and regularly reads from a letter from her husband, killed in World War II: "When it continues like this without letup you learn what it is to really hate. You begin to hate them as a people and want to punish them all—civilians, women, children, old people—it makes no difference, they're all the same, none of them innocent, and for a while your hate and anger keep you from going crazy with fear. But if you let yourself hate and believe in hate, then no matter what else happens, you've lost" (15–16).

The family is surrounded by division and hatred. Michael's mother tells an ugly story of a neighbor's elderly mother, visited in the hospital by her thirteen-year-old grandson Rudy, who is dressed to play for a dance with his rock-and-roll band. The old lady gasps out, "Rudish, you dress like nigger," and falls back dead. "Those aren't the kind of famous last words we're going to hear in this family if I can help it," Michael's mother promises (17).

The cultures meet not only in Michael's mother's tolerance but also in Michael's memories, in which Chopin, Frankie Yankovitch, and boogie-woogie meld in a rich cultural pluralism. It is perhaps a romantic vision of ethnic Chicago but not a sentimental one. Dybek defines it himself in the *TriQuarterly* roundtable:

I keep saying "Chicago tradition," by the way, and maybe ought to try and identify at least some of the aspects I mean by that. It's not just place, local color, but an attitude. For instance, there's a premium placed on a certain kind of savvy—not urbane sophistication—more like street-smarts. . . . In my neighborhood we called it "having the scan." . . . And mixed in with it is another trademark of Chicago writing, one that maybe distinguishes it from other urban traditions, a certain sentimental streak. . . . "Sentimental" is wrong, I should have said "sentiment," or any feeling. You find it clearly in Bellow. The music of the language conveys it. Writers like Bellow and Algren, much more than Farrell, for instance, demonstrate that it's possible to make poetry out of urban dialects and city rhythms. (Gibbons and Shafer 336–37)

This sentiment, a kind of sweetness, runs through Dybek's stories, even when the subject matter is harsh and ugly.

But back to "Blight." At one point in their wanderings, David, Pepper, and Ziggy go over to a viaduct near Douglas Park, "a natural echo chamber where we'd been going for blues-shout contests ever since we'd become infatuated with Screamin' Jay Hawkins's 'I Put a Spell on You'" (46). They stand at the end of the viaduct, beating out the rhythm with a broken automobile antenna, empty bottles, and beer cans and shouting out blues.

> Once, a gang of black kids appeared on the Douglas Park end of the viaduct and stood harmonizing from bass through falsetto just like the Coasters, so sweetly that though at first we tried outshouting them, we finally shut up and listened, except for Pepper keeping the beat.
>
> We applauded from our side but stayed where we were, and they stayed on theirs. Douglas Park had become the new boundary after the riots the summer before.
>
> "How can a place with such good viaducts have blight, man?" Pepper asked, still rapping his aerial as we walked back. (48)

How indeed? The Black kids, David, Pepper, and Ziggy have created a cultural event out of blight. They have made something out of nothing, as Dybek himself does, magnificently, in *The Coast of Chicago*.

The Chicago of Paul Hoover's novel *Saigon, Illinois* (1988) is presented with both a detailed, comic realism and a gradually darkening surrealism, as Chicago life is increasingly colored by the war in Vietnam, reflecting both the narrator's and the nation's guilt. The urban incongruities that give Chernoff's and Dybek's work a magic, fabulist quality are called here into the service of, first, broad comedy and, later, moral commentary.

The narrator is Jim Holder, a member of the pacifist Church of Peace in Malta, Indiana, who refuses to serve in Vietnam, is granted conscientious objector status, and goes to do his alternative service in Metropolitan Hospital in Chicago. The first scene, the hearing before the draft board, sets the tone of broad comedy for the early part of the book. To the question, "What would you do if you were confronted in an alley by a man with a knife?" Holder answers, "I might be aggressively tender." The next question is, "Mr. Holder, are you, or have you ever been . . . a, a, a, . . . homosexual?" Holder replies, "Absolutely not." "A week later," Holder recalls, "I received a letter indicating that I was to work for two years in public service, in a civilian capacity. There was no doubt about my pacifism and no end to the board's bewilderment. They suspected I was queer, but better than that I was odd" (5).

In Chicago, the action moves between the apartment on Halsted Street, near Armitage, which Holder shares with three eccentric roommates, and Metropolitan Hospital, where Holder gets a job as a unit manager. Both worlds are initially presented in the idiom of television comedy. The group at the apartment includes Rose the Poet, who has resigned from his job writing the *Playboy* Advisor column. "The first day of his 'retirement,' he took some speed, wrote thirty poems in two hours, all containing the words *pink* and *electric* in capital letters, and had a nervous breakdown. . . . There was so much residual lysergic acid in Rose's system you could start a car with it if you could get him hooked up to the jumper cables. At least that's what the Selective Service psychologist said when he declared Rose emotionally unfit for the army" (13). Then there are Randy and Penelope. Randy works for Academic Industries, which publishes comic books of classic novels, for adults who are learning to read. He is involved with Anna, a huge woman who takes him to samurai movies and beats him up afterward. Penelope is Australian and walks with a limp for no reason.

The world of the hospital is also comically weird, like a M.A.S.H. on acid. Holder's colleagues are Ed Grabowski, who is working at the hospital as "a kind of a sideline" (40) to his father-in-law's undertaking business, and Barbara Stevens, whose lawyer husband has run off with their "milkman" (female) because he fell in love with her uniform and now lives in a trailer in Albuquerque, where all he does is cook up his special chili.

Even from the beginning, the anarchic comedy of apartment and hospital is undercut by darker undertones. The television news from Vietnam is a recurring, sinister presence, and soon after moving to Chicago, Holder learns of the death of his college roommate, Terry Grubbs, from Tin Cup, Indiana, whose father was a right-wing fanatic and survivalist. Holder's girlfriend Vicki Cepak gets pregnant and undergoes a grisly abortion, they drift apart, and Holder begins an affair with Barbara Stevens. The deaths begin to mount, not only the minutely detailed deaths of terminal patients at the hospital but the deaths of friends and colleagues as well: Martin Baum, another unit manager, who commits suicide with drugs taken from the hospital; Jack Triplett, a tough, redneck paraplegic; and Desiree Hawkins, a hospital station clerk and drug addict, who takes rat poison. The cheerful urban anarchy of the beginning of the novel turns dark and sinister. Holder makes the point explicit in a conversation with Martin Baum:

> I said that I thought that by not going to Vietnam, I would have no contact with death, but every day I carried bodies to the morgue. Sometimes on the el I felt I was choking to death. The other day a drunk woman stood between two moving cars and took off her bra. The train rocketed into the tunnel and she nearly fell, but she caught herself, her broad face smeared against the window. Once a rock flew against the el car window where I was sitting and shattered the glass in a weblike pattern. There were people out there who wanted to do me harm, even though they didn't know me! (128–29)

The problem, the grotesquely fat but wise patient Arnold Feller tells Holder, is that he is caught in a moral contradiction: "The problem with you . . . is that you're trying to be good and bad at the same time. It doesn't usually work out. The best thing is to go to jail. Then the good and bad will be clearer in your mind" (164). Arnold only speaks Holder's own confusion. "You want me to go to jail?" asks Holder. Arnold replies, "That *is* what you want to hear, isn't it?"

Fired from his job only a few weeks before his obligatory service is up and unable to face prison, Holder resorts to flight. He visits his parents' soporific home, pays homage to Terry Grubbs's grave, and drives his barely functioning 1963 Chevy Nova west. The car expires just as he reaches Berkeley. The novel ends ambiguously. Holder goes to the beach, strips, and swims out to sea: "I extended my arms toward an invisible point to the west, and I felt stronger and cleaner, stroke by stroke, a breath at a time" (229). Where is Holder swimming to? To his death? Has the whole novel been a voice from the grave? To Vietnam, his symbolic destination from the beginning? Away from America, which the war and his own conscience have turned into Saigon, Illinois? All are possible in the open, suggestive ending to this wonderful novel.

Four swallows do not make a summer, and four writers cannot represent the full range of Chicago writing in the past twenty years. But Colter, Chernoff, Dybek, and Hoover offer powerful counterexamples to the naturalistic, white, male tradition described so often in our literary histories. The Chicagos they represent are far from simply brutalizing and degrading. They are complex cityscapes, often harsh, it is true, but also often rich, diverse, pluralistic, and full of unexpected wonders. Their atmosphere is not so much the brutal competitiveness the naturalists represented as the combination of urban savvy and sweetness that Dybek describes or that Dave Etter's wry, seasoned prose poem "Chicago" suggests:

> City of the bent shoulders, the bum ticket, the bad back. City of the called third strike, the blocked punt. City of the ever-deferred dream. City of the shattered windshield, the loose wheel, the empty gas tank. City of I remember when, of once upon a time. City of not "I will" but "I wish I could."
>
> (144)

Saul Bellow: Chicago versus the Great Books

By far the fullest and most interesting literary exploration of Chicago, developed over more than forty years, is found in the fiction of Saul Bellow. Bellow's treatment of Chicago is comparable in scale and significance, if not in method, to Dickens's use of London or Joyce's of Dublin. More than setting or even subject, Bellow's Chicago is an imaginative creation that embodies his central themes, a discursive city parallel to the physical one but with a life of its own, the meaning of which cannot be understood merely in terms of documentary accuracy. It is also a diachronic creation, unfolding over time and growing by accretion, so that it might be better to speak of Bellow's Chicagos, a series of representations, each superimposed on the previous ones to produce, progressively and cumulatively, the discursive density of the synchronic Chicago represented by all the novels viewed together.

Regarded merely as documents, Bellow's fictions represent Chicago with a historical and geographic thoroughness, stretching from the 1920s to the 1980s and ranging over the entire city. Joseph, of *Dangling Man* (1944), lives with his wife, Iva, in a single room in a boarding house on the South Side. Joseph sometimes ventures into other parts of the city: the Loop, where he occasionally meets his wife after her work; his in-laws' home in a lower-middle-class neighborhood on the Northwest Side, "a dreary hour's ride on the El" (19); or the prosperous suburb where his stockbroker brother, Amos, lives.

The unities of time and place of *Dangling Man* are exploded in *The Adventures of Augie March* (1953), which treats Chicago, and all else, as sprawling and inconclusive. The March family home is on the Near West Side; they are among only "a handful of Jews" (12) in a predominantly Polish neighborhood. As Augie grows up, his horizons expand to take in the whole city, and the roster of his jobs and residences amounts to an emotional map of Chicago. His first move is to the home of his relatives, the Coblins, who live in a warm, disorderly Jewish neighborhood on the North Side (16). He ventures frequently into the Loop for entertainment and for brief jobs selling newspapers at the La Salle Street station (34) and as a Christmas elf in a department store (43). Einhorn's office and poolroom, which become a second home for Augie for a time, are in the Thirteenth Ward on the West Side. From there, Augie travels into all parts of the city on Einhorn's errands. For a time he is a salesman of luxury items in "the millionaire suburbs—Highland Park, Kenilworth, and Winnetka" (129). For a while he settles in prosperous Evanston as a sporting-goods salesman and protégé of the Renlings. When his arrangement with the Renlings collapses, his fall in status is reflected in a slide down the map of Chicago to a rooming house on the South Side, near the University of Chicago. Augie remains here until he departs for Mexico with Thea, and he settles in the same neighborhood when he returns from Mexico (438). From this base, he ranges out all over the city, trying to sell a wretched rubberized paint (156), picking up dogs from the luxurious homes along the Gold Coast to take to the dog club he works for on North Clark Street (185), and working in his brother's coal yard on the West Side (225).

After *Seize the Day* (1957), set in New York, and *Henderson the Rain King* (1959), largely set in Africa, Bellow returned to a Chicago setting for large portions of *Herzog* (1964), notably Herzog's mad trip to Chicago to "rescue" his daughter Junie. Herzog takes the expressway from O'Hare Airport south to Montrose Avenue and drives southeast on Montrose to the family home on the North Side. Leaving the house, now occupied by his widowed stepmother, Herzog returns to the Edens Expressway and continues south to Congress, where he drives east again to the Outer Drive, along Lake Michigan. He takes the Outer Drive south to the house he occupied with Madeleine, on Harper Avenue in Hyde Park. During Herzog's residence in Chicago, he had taught at "the Downtown College," while Gersbach had been employed as educational director of an FM station in the Loop (6), but both families had lived in the neighborhood of the University of Chicago, the Gersbachs on Woodlawn Avenue. Herzog drives first to Phoebe Gersbach's house and then to Lucas Asphalter's house, also in Hyde Park, where he is to spend the night, stopping to send a telegram to Ramona from the Western Union office at Blackstone and Fifty-third Street (266).

The bathetic climax of Herzog's trip to Chicago takes place in contemporary, public Chicago, in the area of the Loop. Next day, he takes Junie first to the Museum of Science and Industry in Jackson Park and then to the Shedd Aquarium. Leaving the aquarium, he turns south on the Outer Drive to return Junie to Hyde Park, but he is struck by a speeding Volkswagen truck. When the police discover a gun in Herzog's car, he is taken to the police station at Eleventh and State Street.

As Chicago document, *Humboldt's Gift* (1975) ranges widely over the city, though it is centered in its materialistic heart, the Loop. Over and over, Charlie Citrine finds himself hurdling around the Loop's skyscrapers, usually against his will, in the petty mobster Ronald Cantabile's white Thunderbird. In one extended scene, Cantabile and his girlfriend Polly force Citrine and his friend Thaxter into the Thunderbird in front of the Art Institute on Michigan Avenue and take them on a wild tour of Chicago's materialistic center: west on Madison Street, past the lavish Christmas displays of State Street and the "towering upswept frames of the First National Bank" (250), then onto La Salle Street to the Rookery, where Cantabile uses Citrine in a scam to threaten a man named Stronson, who has defrauded a number of investors in hog bellies, cocoa, and gold ore.

From this heart of the moronic, materialistic inferno, where Citrine also confronts his ex-wife's voracious lawyers, he ranges out, sometimes literally, sometimes in memory, to other parts of the city. His luxurious apartment, though not precisely located, is apparently, like Herzog's house, in Hyde Park; when he drives to the Loop he goes north on the Outer Drive past McCormick Place (63). The Russian Bath on Division Street, "near what used to be Robey Street" (now Damen Avenue), where naked old men steam themselves and eat enormous "snacks" (56), is a tender, if comic, evocation of the old immigrants' Chicago that Bellow so often uses as a standard against which to condemn the present: "Things are very elementary here. You feel that these people are almost conscious of obsolescence, of a line of evolution abandoned by nature and culture" (75), like the turtles with whom Herzog identifies in the aquarium. Other centers of nostalgia are in the working-class districts of the Near Northwest Side, where Citrine grew up and went to Chopin School at Rice and Western (90), and the Southwest Side, where his childhood sweetheart Naomi Lutz lives in Marquette Park, again like the Marches, as an isolated Jew in a Catholic, Eastern European neighborhood, in this case Czechoslovakian (287).

The Chicago episodes of *The Dean's December* (1982) range over the entire city, from the Cook County jail and the Cabrini Green housing project to glittering Lakeshore Drive apartments. But they are presented only through the memory of Corde, dean of a university that is unidentified but closely resembles the University of Chicago, and Corde remembers from the perspective of Bucharest, where he has been called to the deathbed of his mother-in-law. It is as if contemporary Chicago were being observed through the wrong end of the Mount Palomar telescope that appears in the last scene of the novel.

This brief inventory of the direct, documentary appearance of Chicago in Bellow's fiction fails to capture the quality of his treatment of the city, less a matter of descriptions of external reality than a prolonged meditation on the meaning of the city, a pervasive transformation of the physical city into discourse. At one point, Corde reflects that he has passed Chicago through his soul: "What you didn't pass through your soul didn't even exist, that was what made the literal literal. Thus he had taken it upon himself to pass Chicago through his own soul. A mass of data, terrible, murderous. It was no easy matter to put such things through. But there was no other way for reality to happen. Reality didn't exist 'out there.' It began to be real only when the soul found its underlying truth. In generalities there was no coherence—none" (266).

Throughout his long career, Bellow—and his various fictional surrogates—have passed Chicago through their souls in this sense. The result cannot be summed up in one of the "generalities" Corde distrusts; it can be understood only by retracing the progressive inscribing of the city, the unfolding discourse, through the novels.

One generality, however, implicit in Corde's meditation, the split between the soul and Chicago, between the mind and the object of its perceptions, is of use in tracing Chicago through the fiction. It is anticipated in *Humboldt's Gift:* "It was now apparent to me that I was neither of Chicago nor sufficiently beyond it, and that Chicago's material and daily interests and phenomena were neither actual and vivid enough nor symbolically clear enough to me. So that I had neither vivid actuality nor symbolic clarity and for the time being I was utterly nowhere" (250–51). The style is Citrine's; the sentiment could be that of any of Bellow's Chicago protagonists, from Joseph in *Dangling Man* onward. Torn between "vivid actuality" and "symbolic clarity" as they contemplate Chicago, they can neither accept it fully in its material reality nor distance themselves from it fully enough to attain symbolic clarity. As they pass Chicago through their souls and make the literal "literal" (not, perhaps, so much "real" as "verbal"), they may find, as Corde does, its "underlying truth," but that truth is not so much unitary, monologic, as it is conflicted, dialogic, torn between the materially vivid and the symbolically clear. Bellow's protagonists are all "dangling men," poised between the fact and the idea.

Bellow's double vision of Chicago (which is, after all, "just the USA," as he says in *Humboldt's Gift* [298]) appears in the pervasive tension in his books between a perceiving consciousness that has behind it the authority of all Western culture, the Great Books, and a perceived reality that, though often debased and vulgar, has a material vitality that resists reduction to a lifeless "symbolic clarity," that refuses to remain mere object to the narrator's subjectivity but talks back, asserting the claims of "vivid actuality." Bellow's most characteristic books are heated, often comic, dialogues between culture, as represented by the Great Books, and the material world, most often represented by Chicago.

The key book in Bellow's inscriptions of Chicago, as in much

else, is *The Adventures of Augie March*. In the first two tentative
"victim" novels—*Dangling Man* and *The Victim* (the latter set in
New York)—the split between the protagonist's mind and the outer
world is expressed in depression and angst. Here is the dangling
man, Joseph, surveying the Chicago cityscape outside his third-floor
window:

> Not far off there were chimneys, their smoke a lighter gray than the
> gray of the sky; and, straight before me, ranges of poor dwellings, ware-
> houses, billboards, culverts, electric signs blankly burning, parked cars
> and moving cars, and the occasional bare plan of a tree. These I sur-
> veyed, pressing my forehead on the glass. It was my painful obligation to
> look and to submit to myself the invariable question: Where was there
> a particle of what, elsewhere, or in the past, had spoken in man's favor?
> There could be no doubt that these billboards, streets, tracks, houses,
> ugly and blind, were related to interior life. And yet, I told myself, there
> had to be a doubt. There were human lives organized around these ways
> and houses, and that they, the houses, say, were the analogue, that what
> men created they also were, through some transcendent means, I could
> not bring myself to concede. There must be a difference, a quality that
> eluded me, somehow, a difference between things and persons and even
> between acts and persons. Otherwise the people who lived here were
> actually a reflection of the things they lived among. (24–25)

Joseph's painful attempt to "read" the enigmatic Chicago landscape is echoed, with an affirmation perhaps more desperate than
genuine, in "Looking for Mr. Green." Grebe, trying to deliver relief
checks in the icy, crumbling Black ghetto, realizes that his task is
fundamentally hermeneutic; he "needed experience in interpreting
looks and signs" (88). The problem is to find the language that will
unlock the meaning of the ghetto. The story is full of languages
and inscriptions; Grebe has a classical education, and he and his
supervisor Raynor, a law graduate, joke in French and trade Latin
tags. Their assumptions are Platonic; their humanistic educations
have amounted to "permission to go and find out what were the last
things that everything stands for while everybody else labored in the
fallen world of appearances" (96).

In the course of the story, the elusive Mr. Green becomes the
last thing that everything stands for. But between Green and Grebe
stand problems of interpretation for which Grebe's education has
not prepared him. He must read the minute shifts in expression and

the guarded comments of the distrustful ghetto dwellers whom he asks for directions, and he must translate their graphic equivalents scrawled on the decaying walls: "WHOODY-DOODY GO TO JESUS, and zigzags, caricatures, sexual scrawls, and curses" (90). The ghetto presents a challenge in identifying the "natural," which, if not unique to Chicago, is exacerbated there:

> Objects once so new, so concrete that it could never have occurred to anyone they stood for other things, had crumbled. Therefore, reflected Grebe, the secret of them was out. It was that they stood for themselves by agreement, and were natural and not unnatural by agreement, and when the things themselves collapsed the agreement became visible. What was it, otherwise, that kept cities from looking peculiar? Rome, that was almost permanent, did not give rise to thoughts like these. And was it abidingly real? But in Chicago, where the cycles were so fast and the familiar died out, and again rose changed, and died again in thirty years, you saw the common agreement or covenant, and you were forced to think about appearances and realities. (104–5)

To find the reality behind appearances finally boils down in the story to a question of naming. The dignified old man, Winston Field, whom Grebe seeks out, temporarily frustrated in his quest for Green, insists on establishing his name with a whole boxful of identity cards. "You got to know who I am," he tells Grebe (101). And Grebe tells one of his reluctant informants: "It almost doesn't do any good to have a name if you can't be found by it. It doesn't stand for anything. He might as well not have any" (106–7).

Grebe finally finds what may be Mr. Green's house, but there he encounters not Mr. Green but an enormous, naked, drunken woman, who replies, when he asks if she is Mrs. Green, only, "Maybe I is, and maybe I ain't" (108). Grebe rather optimistically delivers the check to her: "Though she might not be Mrs. Green, he was convinced that Mr. Green was upstairs. Whoever she was, the woman stood for Green, whom he was not to see this time" (109). The story ends with Grebe elated: "For after all he *could* be found!" (109). But could he? In taking the doubtful name "Mrs. Green" to stand for the naked woman who in turn stands for Mr. Green, Grebe has perhaps stopped several layers short in the world of "hostile appearances" of "the last thing that everything stands for" and has bridged the gap only with wishful thinking.

The main outlines of Bellow's readings of Chicago—the cultured observer, the brutal material world, and the futile attempt to bridge the gap between the two—are already present in *Dangling Man* and "Looking for Mr. Green." What separates them from the mature Bellow, whose voice is first heard in *The Adventures of Augie March,* is what Augie himself calls "larkiness" (12). The early victim fiction is not without a certain sardonic humor, but nothing in it prepares us for the comic voice of *Augie March:* "I am an American, Chicago born—Chicago, that somber city—and go at things as I have taught myself, free-style, and will make the record in my own way: first to knock, first admitted; sometimes an innocent knock, sometimes a not so innocent. But a man's character is his fate, says Heraclitus, and in the end there isn't any way to disguise the nature of the knocks by acoustical work on the door or gloving the knuckles" (3).

Much could be said (and has been said) about this famous opening; perhaps the simplest is that it creates a voice that can move without strain from Chicago to Heraclitus and back again. Joseph and Grebe, too, view Chicago from the perspective of European humanism, but they are dangling outsiders, thrown onto the streets of Chicago by the depression and war, and are provided with academic vitae to rationalize their cultured perspectives. Augie, by contrast, is of Chicago; his inner life is fundamentally a reflection of the drab city streets that Joseph lamented. His bookishness, the ease with which he can drop Heraclitus into his paragraph, creates a perspective on Chicago that is the source not of plangent lament but of boisterous comedy.

Augie's language, too, is of Chicago, in a way that Joseph's and Grebe's are not, not a transcription of Chicago speech but a language that reflects the looseness of controls, the openness to contingency, of Augie's own life. In that first sentence, Augie is making the record in his own way: not just his life but the narrative of his life, the book we are beginning. He does it "free-style," in a string of loosely connected clauses and phrases that anticipates the serial construction of the narrative it begins.

But is Heraclitus right? Is a man's character his fate, or is his fate—to be an American, Chicago born—his character? Augie is no more sure than Joseph is of the relationship between the self and the world, of the degree to which people "were actually a reflection of the things they lived among." Within a few pages, Augie, who begins the book by asserting the supremacy of his own will, acknowledges that his will is itself the product of what he has grown up among: "All the influences were lined up waiting for me. I was born, and there they were to form me, which is why I tell you more of them than of myself" (43).

The question of the relation of self and world, and specifically the world of Chicago, is not one that can be answered, but it provides the focus for Augie's continuing exploration of his own development, what it means to grow up in this "Ezekiel caldron of wrath, stoked with bones" (458). What does it mean to grow up in an environment that does not offer the pastoral fantasy of childhood as "silken, unconscious, nature-painted times"?

> But when there is no shepherd-Sicily, no free-hand nature-painting, but deep city vexation instead, and you are forced early into deep city aims, not sent in your ephod before Eli to start service in the temple, nor set on a horse by your weeping sisters to go and study Greek in Bogota, but land in a poolroom—what can that lead to of the highest? And what happiness or misery-antidote can it offer instead of pipes and sheep or musical, milk-drinking innocence, or even merely nature walks with a pasty instructor in goggles, or fiddle lessons? Friends, human pals, men and brethren, there is no brief, digest, or shorthand way to say where it leads. Crusoe, alone with nature, under heaven, had a busy, complicated time of it with the inhuman itself, and I am in a crowd that yields results with much more difficulty and reluctance and am part of it myself. (84–85)

In a sense, the style of this passage answers its own question; a childhood of "deep city vexation" cannot be absolutely disastrous if it produces a sensibility capable of sentences like these. Their effect, like that of the book itself, is the product of the sureness of management of a comic-ironic tone. This is mock-epic: the treatment of the mean materiality of a Chicago poolroom from the perspective of the Great Books. Unlike Joseph, however, Augie does not ally himself unreservedly with the Great Books and contemplate Chicago with a self-pitying despair. Augie's Great Books are themselves somewhat comically undercut, because they are such a higgledy-piggledy assortment of Alexandrian romance, the Old Testament, *The Bridge of San Luis Rey,* and *Robinson Crusoe.* Moreover, the street energy of Augie's language—free-style, as he has taught himself—asserts the claims of material Chicago against high-culture fantasy. In this dialogic encounter of the Great Books with Chicago, each comments on the other, with Augie hovering as comic mediator between the two.

The joke never wears thin in *Augie March.* Here is Augie carrying the paralyzed Einhorn up the steps to the third-floor whorehouse, where Einhorn is going to give Augie his rather unconventional high-school graduation gift: "I stopped the car and went out to scout, came back when I had found the joint, and got him on my back. He used to talk about himself as the Old Man of the Sea riding Sinbad. But there was Aeneas too, who carried his old dad Anchises in the burning of Troy, and that old man had been picked by Venus to be her lover; which strikes me as the better comparison" (122). Can "deep city aims," like an incongruous visit to a Chicago whorehouse, be usefully treated in terms of the *Thousand and One Nights* and the *Aeneid*? Possible parallels are struck off almost in passing: Augie as both Sinbad and Aeneas, irresponsible adventurer and culture hero; Einhorn as simultaneously incubus, generous father-surrogate, and sexual model; Chicago as Troy. Even to mention the possibilities seems too serious; the real point seems to be the comic disjunction between the two orders of discourse, the dialogue between high culture and modern, urban experience.

Augie March, taken as a whole, offers at least an oblique answer to Joseph's question as to where there was in Chicago anything that "elsewhere, or in the past, had spoken in man's favor," and even Augie's as to what a Chicago childhood, in "deep city vexation," could "lead to of the highest." Augie's mature voice in the novel confirms Joseph's hopes that people may not be merely "a reflection of the things they lived among." If the running high-culture allusions and analogues provide a reminder of traditional high conceptions of humanity and the Chicago street scenes represent contemporary material reality, reality does not necessarily come in second best. Augie survives and even prevails not by the Great Books but by street smarts, by a tough refusal to be recruited to anyone else's version of what is real (402) and by an insistence on holding out for "a fate good enough" (318).

Augie March is full of world-makers: people who project their perceptions of reality into entire worlds and try to recruit others to inhabit those worlds. In Mexico, Augie finds in his and Thea's rented house a battered anthology of literary utopias: "It contained Campanella's *City of the Sun,* More's *Utopia,* Machiavelli's *Discourses* and *The Prince,* as well as long selections from St. Simon, Comte, Marx and Engels" (356). Augie is fascinated by the book, reads it straight through, and reflects on the competition between private inventions of the world:

The great chiefs and leaders recruit the greatest number, and that's what their power is. There's one image that gets out in front to lead the rest and can impose its claim to being genuine with more force than others, or one voice enlarged to thunder is heard above the others. Then a huge invention, which is the invention maybe of the world itself, and of nature, becomes the actual world—with cities, factories, public buildings, railroads, armies, dams, prisons, and movies—becomes the actuality. That's the struggle of humanity, to recruit others to your version of what's real. Then even the flowers and the moss on the stones become the moss and the flowers of a version. (402)

The function of Chicago for Augie, and for the book, is to serve as a touchstone of reality against which to measure these invented worlds. Of course Augie's Chicago is no more real than anyone else's version of bedrock reality. Based, like theirs, on a particular definition of what it is to be human (and perhaps an especially low one), it is merely what Augie constructs as his reality.

This perception is shared by Moses Herzog, for whom Chicago also represents the primary reality. On his outing in Chicago with Junie, Herzog realizes that in his "near-delirium" he perceives his surroundings very personally, "as though he painted them with moisture and color taken from his own mouth, his blood, liver, bowels, genitals":

> In this mingled way, therefore, he was aware of Chicago, familiar ground to him for more than thirty years. And out of its elements, by this peculiar art of his own organs, he created his version of it. Where the thick walls and buckled slabs of pavement in the Negro slums exhaled their bad smells. Farther West, the industries; the sluggish South branch dense with sewage and glittering with a crust of golden slime; the Stockyards, deserted; the tall red slaughterhouses in lonely decay; and then a faintly buzzing dullness of bungalows and scrawny parks; and vast shopping centers; and the cemeteries after these—Waldheim, with its graves for Herzogs past and present; the Forest Preserves for riding parties, Croatian picnics, lovers' lanes, horrible murders; airports; quarries; and, last of all, cornfields. And with this, infinite forms of activity—Reality. Moses had to see reality. (278)

This remarkable passage, like *Herzog* as a whole, rocks between the twin poles of self and world. Chicago, at the beginning of the passage, is Herzog's "version" of it, created by the "peculiar art of his own organs." (And this Chicago is a comic projection of the depressive Herzog's own preoccupations, full of slaughterhouses, cemeteries of dead Herzogs, and forest preserves set aside for Croatian picnics and horrible murders.) By the end of the passage, the Herzogian version of Chicago has become not just real but "Reality" itself. The "invention," in Augie March's terms, has become the "actuality."

Herzog, like *Augie March,* is peopled with world-builders or, as they are called here, reality instructors: *"A very special sort of lunatic expects to inculcate his principles.* Sandor Himmelstein, Valentine Gersbach, Madeleine P. Herzog, Moses himself. Reality instructors. *They want to teach you—to punish you with—the lessons of the Real"* (125; italics are Bellow's and indicate Herzog's running inner "text"). Significantly, Herzog includes himself among this very special sort of lunatic, echoing the opening line of the book: "If I am out of my mind, it's all right with me, thought Moses Herzog" (1).

Reality is the issue in *Herzog.* The "realities" of Himmelstein, Gersbach, and Madeleine are no realities at all but versions to which they forcefully try to recruit others. Herzog's particular kind of lunacy is to retreat from the bombardment of others' "realities" into a fuguelike, freewheeling inner monologue punctuated by his painful, comic letters, none sent, most not even written down, beginning with his mother (*"As to why I haven't visited your grave in so long . . ."* [11]), continuing through friends, public figures, and great thinkers of the past (*"Dear Herr Nietzsche—My dear sir, May I ask a question from the floor?"* [318–19]), and ending with God ("To God he jotted several lines" [325]). The Great Books are not the cause of Herzog's madness, but they provide the form the symptoms take, as he himself ironically acknowledges: "I'm bugging all these people— Nehru, Churchill, and now Ike, whom I apparently want to give a Great Books course" (162).

Herzog is caught in a world of letters, not just his obsessive imaginary correspondence but language itself, that of others as well as his own. The problem with the "lessons of the Real" that others try to impose on him and that he imposes on both himself and others is not that they are not valid, in their own ways, but that they have lost any significant relationship with experience. The book is full of talkers whose words are ironically contradicted by their experiential context: Shapiro, whose discourse on Russian mysticism is undercut by his "snarling teeth, his salivating greed, the dagger of an ulcer in his belly" (77), or Himmelstein, whose presumed solicitude for Junie is juxtaposed with his profane rage at his own daughters: "Spendthrift bitches! Frigging lice! All they're good for is to wag their asses at the dress shops and play gidgy in the bushes. Then they come home, and gorge cake and leave plates smeared with chocolate in the sink" (88–89). Herzog's own most serious excursion into world building is his theory that Madeleine and Gersbach are abusing Junie, elaborated, significantly, from a letter, one from a graduate student and baby-sitter named Geraldine Portnoy, who tells him of seeing Junie locked in Gersbach's car and crying while Madeleine and Gersbach quarrel indoors.

This illusion is not shattered until Herzog flies to Chicago, determined to kill Gersbach, and stands on a cement block outside the bathroom window of Madeleine's house and watches Gersbach tenderly bathe Junie: "As soon as Herzog saw the actual person giving an actual bath, the reality of it, the tenderness of such a buffoon to a little child, his intended violence turned into theater, into something ludicrous. He was not ready to make such a complete fool of himself" (258). The "reality" of the bath scene is different from the "reality" advanced by the reality instructors, including Herzog himself.

Commentators on *Herzog* have perhaps neglected this scene and placed too much importance on the final one, in which Herzog achieves a sort of silent transcendence in the heart of the natural world in Ludeyville, especially regarding the central issue of whether or not Herzog manages to liberate himself by the last page from the madness he announces on the first. John J. Clayton has argued most forcefully that he does not, finding in Ludeyville only a temporary retreat from neurosis rather than a resolution of it, while Judie Newman has argued very convincingly that he does, seeing Ludeyville not as a timeless Eden but as the place where Herzog stops his psychic flight into world-historical problems and accepts responsibility for his own history.

I would agree with Newman but would locate the turning point not in Ludeyville but on that cement block outside the bathroom window. That moment, significantly a silent one, is set in a rich context of corrective reality. Herzog's flight to Chicago is a flight not from reality but into reality, not only present experience but his own past: being sexually abused as a child by a strange man (288), being threatened by his father with the same pistol he plans to shoot

Gersbach with (250), and losing Madeleine to Gersbach. Herzog's "clumsy, stinking, tender Chicago" (242) may be only a version of reality, but it is his reality, and it is here that Herzog finally begins to find some relationship between the "symbolic clarity" of his ideas and the "vivid actuality" of the material world. The rest of the novel is a working out of that relationship, ending in the final silent moment when Herzog "had no messages for anyone. Nothing. Not a single word" (341).

Chicago appears to be an inexhaustible subject for Bellow; its prominence in the action of *Humboldt's Gift* and *The Dean's December,* noted earlier, is matched by its thematic centrality in these novels. If Chicago is represented ambivalently in the earlier books, however—split between nostalgia for childhood life in warm ethnic neighborhoods and revulsion for the city's brute materiality—the balance swings heavily toward the latter in these later novels. A touch of Herzog's sense that his neighborhood childhood is especially privileged as "real" survives in Charlie Citrine's nostalgia for his high-school sweetheart Naomi Lutz and his feeling that if he could have embraced her "every night for forty years, as her husband, of course," his life would have been "completely fulfilled, a success—instead of this" (280). But Citrine thinks more about today's Chicago than yesterday's, and Albert Corde, of *The Dean's December,* has no nostalgia for old Chicago at all.

Bellow is fond of planting in his novels reflexive descriptions of themselves. Thus *Herzog,* about a man whose inner life consists of a series of letters, is itself a series of letters, and Herzog finds that he has nothing more to say, "not a single word," at precisely the point that his creator does. This painter-in-the-mirror effect appears in *Humboldt's Gift* in Charlie Citrine's description of *Caldofreddo,* the screenplay on which he and Humboldt once collaborated: "And we saw the movie as a vaudeville and farce but with elements of Oedipus at Colonus in it. Violent spectacular sinners in old age acquire magical properties, and when they come to die they have the power to curse and bless" (175). *Humboldt's Gift* is certainly vaudeville and farce; the ambiguity is who the violent spectacular sinner in old age is. Humboldt himself fits the bill, and he has the power to curse and bless, directly through his legacy "gift" of the screenplay, more generally through his poetic "gift." Citrine himself is also an aged Oedipus caught up in a farce. He has plenty of violent, spectacular sins in his past, too; he is obsessed with encroaching age (whereas Humboldt died comparatively young); and his tone, as he surveys the "moronic inferno" (34) of America, is jeremiadical, sometimes comically so, sometimes not.

This double reference is consistent with the novel as a whole, which throughout presents Humboldt as Citrine's double. Bellow's dualistic vision persistently finds expression in splittings, pairings, and binaries of various sorts, but *Humboldt's Gift* is his fullest exploration of the double since *The Victim*. Humboldt was a romantic, a poet, Citrine is an ironist, a historian; Humboldt went under, Citrine survived; Humboldt died a pauper, Citrine is rich. Each has fictionalized the other; Citrine has borrowed Humboldt's flamboyant personality for his Broadway hit *Von Trenck*, while Humboldt has slyly captured Citrine's role as "farcical martyr" in his "Corcoran" screenplay (332–35).

Not the least of these symmetries and contrasts is the fact that Humboldt has made New York his professional home, while Citrine has based himself in Chicago. This contrast is thematized, along with several others, in the second paragraph of the novel, when Citrine remembers Humboldt saying about him, "There's something perverse with that guy. After making this dough why does he bury himself in the sticks? What's he in Chicago for? He's afraid to be found out" (2). The answer to the question of why Citrine remains in Chicago is more complex than merely trying to escape evaluation by living in a second-rate place, and much of the rest of the novel is devoted to exploring Citrine's attachment to Chicago and its relevance to the theme of the poet in America.

Citrine does not remain in Chicago out of any affection for it in any ordinary sense. His attitude toward the city has more than a touch of Pat Colander's "Second City voodoo," a wry, comic pride in the city's ugliness and corruption. When he visits Humboldt's dreadful rural retreat in New Jersey, where "the very bushes might have been on welfare," he can find a touch of charm in the scene because, he says, "I was trained in Chicago to make something of such a scant setting. In Chicago you become a connoisseur of the near-nothing" (23). "There were beautiful and moving things in Chicago," he reflects, "but culture was not one of them. What we had was a cultureless city pervaded nevertheless by Mind" (66). Examining stolen goods in an elegant apartment in the Hancock

Building with Ronald Cantabile, Citrine feels "the need to laugh rising, mounting, always a sign that my weakness for the sensational, my American, Chicagoan (as well as personal) craving for high stimuli, for incongruities and extremes, was aroused. . . . Such information about corruption, if you had grown up in Chicago, was easy to accept. It even satisfied a certain need. It harmonized with one's Chicago view of society" (95).

Aside from his Second City joking, there are personal reasons for Citrine to remain in Chicago. Just as the title of Herzog's book, *Romanticism and Christianity* (6), touched, both seriously and comically, on two of his problems, so Citrine is working on a book that seems to engage both professional and personal concerns:

> a very personal overview of the Intellectual Comedy of the modern mind. No one person could do this comprehensively. By the end of the nineteenth century what had been the ample novels of Balzac's Comedy had already been reduced to stories by Chekhov in his Russian *Comedie Humaine*. Now it's even less possible to be comprehensive. I never had a work of fiction in mind but a different kind of imaginative projection. Different also from Whitehead's *Adventures of Ideas.* . . . This is not the moment to explain it. (70; Bellow's ellipses)

Humboldt's Gift is itself this "Intellectual Comedy of the modern mind." Bellow can write it; for Citrine it remains only a series of notes and memos kept in a locked drawer of his desk, "many of them written under the influence of liquor" (70). Perhaps, like Herzog blocking on his second book about "how life could be lived by renewing universal connections" (39), Citrine cannot finish his book because he is too busy living it and carrying on a running interior philosophical commentary on his experiences.

For Citrine, Chicago is the perfect setting for writing his modern intellectual human comedy, as he explains in describing another of his abortive works:

> I may as well admit that I came back to settle in Chicago with the secret motive of writing a significant work. This lethargy of mine is related to that project—I got the idea of doing something with the chronic war between sleep and consciousness that goes on in human nature. My subject, in the final Eisenhower years, was boredom. Chicago was the ideal place in which to write my master essay—"Boredom." In raw Chicago you could examine the human spirit under industrialism. (104)

Chicago, after all, is "just the USA" (298), taking American materiality to its unfettered extreme. Chicago, "with its gigantesque outer life contained the whole problem of poetry and the inner life in America" (9).

Citrine, however, never writes his study of "the human spirit under industrialism" or his modern human comedy because he finds that he is "neither of Chicago nor sufficiently beyond it"; he can achieve neither "vivid actuality nor symbolic clarity" and so is "utterly nowhere" (250–51). The truth is that Citrine, for all his praise of the inner life, is irresistibly drawn toward the outer life as well, and much of the energy of the book comes from the flamboyant agents of "materiality" who parade through it, especially Ronald (or Rinaldo) Cantabile, the petty gangster whose assault on Citrine's Mercedes initially propels him into the "moronic inferno." For all Citrine's distaste for him, Cantabile is as much a double for Citrine as Humboldt is. They have in common flashy clothes, colorful sexual lives, and a fascination with Chicago. Citrine is figuratively poised between Humboldt and Cantabile as Renata is torn between her intellectual lover, Citrine, and her undertaker one, Flonzaley. Together, Humboldt and Cantabile express the divisions of Citrine's character: poet versus gangster, the inner life versus the outer life, the Great Books versus Chicago.

Humboldt's Gift itself is divided in the same way. Bellow locates himself in the same discursive space as Citrine: between the intellectual and the material, culture and immediate experience, "symbolic clarity" and "vivid actuality." The result is a brilliant dialogic novel that generates comedy out of Citrine's "inner civil war versus the open life which is elementary, easy for everyone to read, and characteristic of this place, Chicago, Illinois" (270).

Both as a work of art and as an interpretation of Chicago, *The Dean's December* represents a radical shift of direction for Bellow. Martin Amis sees the novel as inaugurating a new phase in Bellow's work, which he calls "Late Bellow," extended in *Him with His Foot in His Mouth* (1984). It is concerned, he says, with "last things, leavetaking, and final lucidities" and is marked by "a more formal artistry, with sharper focus, a keener sense of pattern and balance," as well as by "a countervailing ferocity in his apprehension of the peculiar disorders and distortions of the modern era" (8). Amis terms these qualities "Yeatsian" (10), an accurate term that might be extended not only to the lucidity, artistry, and ferocity but to the social and political views as well.

If the letters in *Herzog* and the Caldofreddo screenplay in *Humboldt's Gift* are embedded texts that mirror the structures of the novels in which they appear, their parallel in *The Dean's December* is the series of controversial articles about Chicago that Corde has published in *Harper's* magazine. Amis sees these articles as "a preemptive strike for the novel itself" (6); in defending them within the novel, Corde/Bellow can at the same time defend the novel, which has a similar import. The actual contents of these articles are only gradually and fragmentarily revealed through the course of the novel, always surrounded by the Dean's memories and second thoughts and sometimes given only in summary. The subject of the articles is the Black underclass in Chicago. They were originally intended to be quite innocuous—"period pieces, picturesque, charming, nostalgic"—but, in the process of writing, "his essays somehow got out of hand" (101). He "gave up his cover, ran out, swung wild at everyone, made enemies" (69). "Something went wrong," Corde reflects. "He wrote about whirling souls and became a whirling soul himself, lifted up, caught up, spinning, streaming with passions, compulsive protests, inspirations. He experienced, as he saw when he looked back, a kind of air anarchy. . . . Because of the incompleteness of his argument he confused many readers. Some wrote contemptuously, others were incensed. He hadn't meant to make such a stir. It took him by surprise" (193).

The actual content of the articles seems to have been a series of vignettes of contemporary Chicago: an interview with Rufus Ridpath, a Black who cleaned up the county jail but has been railroaded on a charge of abusing prisoners; another with Toby Winthrop, also Black, an ex-hit man who operates a successful drug-treatment center on the South Side; an account of a sadistic rape and murder case and an interview with the liberal public defender representing the accused, a Black named Spofford Mitchell; tales of visits to the public housing projects Cabrini Green and the Robert Taylor Homes; an account of the dialysis unit in the Cook County Hospital; sketches of visits to courts trying mainly Black offenders; and descriptions of "broad-daylight rapes and robberies, sexual acts in public places, on the seats of CTA buses, on the floors of public waiting rooms, men on Sheridan Road spraying automobile fenders with their urine" (162).

What is less clear from these fragments are the conclusions that Corde has drawn from all this. He admits, in retrospect, that the tone was "highly nervous, ragged, wild, uncontrolled, turbulent" (152), and that "there was a sort of anarchy in the feelings with which those sketches were infused, an uncontrolled flow of 'poetry,' the truth-passion he had taken into his veins as an adolescent" (180). He seems to have accused the political establishment of regarding the underclasses as "superfluous populations" isolated and left to kill themselves off through drugs and crime (192). He has also attacked the media and the universities. Dewey Spangler summarizes Corde's concerns:

> If [Corde] emphasizes strongly the sufferings of urban populations, especially in the ghettos, it is because he thinks that public discussion is threadbare, that this is either the cause or the effect of blindness (or both the cause and effect) and that our cultural poverty has the same root as the frantic and criminal life of our once great cities. He blames the communications industry for this. It breeds hysteria and misunderstanding. He also blames the universities. Academics have made no effort to lead the public. The intellectuals have been incapable of clarifying our principal problems and of depicting democracy to itself in this time of agonized struggle. (301)

The tone of the articles also has aroused opposition. Spangler tells Corde that he made them sound "like a visionary project, or the voice of God saying, 'Write this up, as follows'" (243–44). The articles have been apocalyptic, as Spangler says (perhaps exaggerating somewhat): "It was when you got apocalyptic about it that you lost me: the dragon coming out of the abyss, the sun turning black like sackcloth, the heavens rolled up like a scroll, Death on his ashen horse. Wow! You sounded like the Reverend Jones of Jonestown" (246).

The most serious of the charges against the articles, though it is not directly confronted, is that they are racist. Corde seems to have gone out of his way to present the underclass as victims rather than predators and to present two strong Black reformers, Ridpath and Winthrop. These, however, do not seem to have balanced the horrifying circumstances of the Spofford Mitchell murder case, the episode in Cabrini Green in which "some man had butchered a hog in his apartment and had thrown the guts on the staircase, where a woman, slipping on them, had broken her arm, and screamed curses in the ambulance" (131), and the inferno of the Chicago courts, "a wilderness wilder than the Guiana bush" (158). Corde's charges against the Blacks seem to be that they have "no sense of place" (237), unlike the earlier immigrants in "the good old days when Chicago was a city of immigrants who had found work, food and freedom and a kind of friendly ugliness around them" (238). The idea that there is a Black culture distinct from white, Western culture he dismisses with contempt: "There is no culture there, it's only a wilderness, and damn monstrous, too" (206). It is these elements in the articles that have led the student radical group to pass a resolution declaring that Corde is a racist and "that he owed a public apology 'to Black, Puerto Rican and Mexican toilers' for making them look 'like animals and savages'" (163).

Corde himself, in reconsidering the articles, seems to place most emphasis not on particular judgments but on their call to redefine the terms in which public questions are considered, to bring the perspective of humane culture to bear upon them. In remembering his hostile interview with his radical nephew, Mason, Corde recalls how "he had wanted to open his heart to Mason, to tell him that under the present manner of interpretation people were shadows to one another, and shadows within shadows, to suggest that these appalling shadows *condemned* our habitual manner of interpretation" (78). He has tried to say "what the human meaning of this decay was and what it augured for civilization" (303).

The relationship between the *Harper's* articles and *The Dean's December*, in which they are embedded, is complex and ingenious. Even Corde's name may suggest that Bellow is attempting to "open his heart" (Latin *cor*), as Corde longs to do to Mason, in explaining the basis of his political positions. Bellow places the main action of the novel in Bucharest, where Corde has gone with his new wife, Minna, to visit her mother on her deathbed. Hot, capitalistic Chicago and cold, Communist Bucharest are balanced; Dewey Spangler, with his journalist's unerring ear for the hackneyed, calls his column on Corde "A Tale of Two Cities" (298). If Chicago is spinning out of control and on the brink of apocalypse, the icy, total bureaucratic control that has followed revolution in Bucharest is not an acceptable alternative. Bucharest also provides a geographical equivalent of the emotional distance Corde tries to place between himself and the articles and their reception. Corde thus has two "voices" in the novel, that of the articles, caught up in Chicago's moronic inferno, and that of his present self, contemplating the articles after several months and from another continent.

These voices are not in debate, however; Corde in contemplation thinks the same as Corde in controversy, and the present events of the novel only confirm his judgments. The underclass he describes in the articles has taken its toll in his college just before his departure. Two Blacks have killed a student, and Corde has braved liberal opposition to raise a reward to bring them to strict justice; they are convicted while Corde is abroad. The media and the academics he condemned in the articles reappear in the persons of the meretricious journalist, Dewey Spangler, and the equally meretricious provost, Alec Witt. In unholy though unwitting alliance, they destroy Corde, Spangler attacking him in a slyly contemptuous column and Witt firing him because Spangler quotes Corde as attacking academic tenure as "the higher welfare" (303).

Critics of the articles, and presumably of *The Dean's December,* by "pre-emptive strike," as Amis would have it, are disarmed by being represented both in letters of protest over the *Harper's* articles and in the other characters of the novel. The letters are simplistic and self-serving; Corde is attacked as naive, elitist, and mad, and his cultural pretensions are lampooned: "Mr. Corde believes in gemütlichkeit more than in public welfare. And what makes him think that what it takes to save little black kids is to get them to read Shakespeare? Next he will suggest that we teach them Demosthenes and make speeches in Greek. The answer to juvenile crime is not in *King Lear* or *Macbeth*" (187).

Of the critics of the articles among the characters of the novel, Minna, Corde's wife, is treated most gently; as an astronomer who soars above the mundane earth (like Thea in *Augie March*), she simply doesn't understand. But Mason Zaehner, Corde's dreadful nephew; Dewey Spangler; and Alec Witt are savage caricatures of Corde's critics: student radicals, journalists, and academics.

The apocalyptic note in the articles—the "dragon coming out of the abyss" (246) and so forth—is sounded also in the frame story.

"Here was an apocalypse—yet another apocalypse to set before the public," Corde muses when he is asked to write a series of articles setting forth Professor Beech's theory that the world is dying of lead poisoning (140). After Corde and his wife return to Chicago, they attend a lavish birthday party for a dog, the Book of Revelation reset in a Lakeshore Drive high-rise apartment: "Yes, decadence, of course, Corde supposed, though he was almost certainly the only one who supposed it. An all-but-derelict civilization? And the dog, if he represented the Great Beast of the Apocalypse, was also the pal of the Sorokins, on whom the blond wife doted" (294). The novel ends inside the dome of the Mount Palomar telescope. Corde has accompanied his wife to the observation cage, and as he descends in the elevator, he regrets, despite the cold of the heavens, having to return to earth: "I almost think I mind coming down more" (312). The telescope itself is perhaps Yeats's "cold eye / On life, on death," and the world-weary Corde feels its strong attraction.

The Dean's December is, to date, Bellow's fullest inscription of Chicago. (Chicago sometimes serves as setting but never as theme in *Him with His Foot in His Mouth* [1984], *More Die of Heartbreak* [1987], and *A Theft* [1989].) It clearly continues his earlier treatments of the city in presenting Chicago as an extreme representative of American culture, in its nostalgia for the old ethnic neighborhoods, and in the opposition it sets up between material urban reality and Western culture: Chicago versus the Great Books. What is new is the savagery with which it attacks material reality; Bellow cannot extend to the Black community the same appreciation of warmth, vitality, and openness that he drew on in describing the immigrant neighborhoods in *Augie March, Herzog,* and *Humboldt's Gift.*

The Dean's December is a beautifully constructed novel that fully merits Amis's praise of its "sense of pattern and balance." It is also a courageous book, one of the few pieces of fiction that explore seriously the meaning of ghettos like the South Side of Chicago in American life. What limits its power is that, just as it mirrors the embedded magazine articles in action, theme, and tone, so it duplicates their journalistic nature. The novel seems thin because only one voice is heard, though that voice is heard twice. It is monologic and so misses the richness of Bellow's earlier Chicago novels that debated so honestly, and so comically, the relative claims of "vivid actuality" and "symbolic clarity."

In the special Chicago issue of *TriQuarterly,* the fine Chicago novelist Richard Stern has one of his characters say:

> Like most Chicagoans, I'm insouciant about the ubiquitous payoffs which oil city life, proud as the next non-insider about the city's reputation: frauds, clout, Rat-a-tat-tat, Fast Eddies, Bathhouse Johns, Needlenose Labriolas, Don't-Make-No-Waves. Chicago's the country's real Disneyland, Oberammergau with real nails. For us, California's just Polynesia on wheels and the Sun Belt won't hold up anyone's pants. Since Mrs. O'Leary, our writers have been feeding this guff to the world, and to us. Even the best Chicago politician knows he doesn't have a chance here unless he at least pretends to know this old score, winking and smiling, even if he never dreamed of taking an illicit nickel. (Gibbons and Shafer, 185)

Much of Chicago's history has been raw, brutal, and corrupt, and its literature has often reflected those qualities. But when history operates to privilege only one kind of experience as "real" and censors out counterexamples, it turns into "guff." Hogbutcher Chicago has passed into myth and is available to writers only for irony and comedy, as it is for Stern, for Mike Royko in his Slats Grobnik sketches, and, if the truth be told, for Saul Bellow. Any persuasive account of Chicago's literature must allow for Elia Peattie as well as Frank Norris, Studs Terkel as well as Nelson Algren, and Cyrus Colter as well as James T. Farrell.

This book has tended to swing, perhaps rather disconcertingly, between close readings of various texts, sometimes rather obscure ones, and sweeping generalizations about the quality of American life. The gap seems wide, and yet it can be bridged.

We Illinoisans have mixed feelings about our home. On the one hand, we feel that the Midwest is somehow the most "American" of the regions of the United States, where sturdy American values survive, far from the excesses of the decadent East Coast and the psychedelic West Coast. We have a sense, sometimes a confused and sentimental one, that Lincoln personifies our earthy, democratic power. We are proud of our wealth, our miles of grain-filled fields and the glitter of Michigan Avenue, and perhaps half-consciously feel that it is our just reward for keeping the democratic faith. On the other hand, we know our great, monotonous spaces make outsiders think of Illinois as "fly-over country," we are aware that all over the world the emblem of Chicago is not the Art Institute but the Thompson submachine gun, and we are ashamed of our burgeoning slums (more than ashamed if we live in them).

By tracing the development of the principal metonyms of Illinois, this book has tried to touch on how this guarded, ambivalent way of looking at Illinois came about. Most Illinoisans, of course, have never read Carl Sandburg or Saul Bellow, much less Eliza Farnham or Thorstein Veblen; their sense of their home comes from the quality of their day-to-day experience rather than from books. Yet even that experience has been shaped by words, the mountains of discourse that have accumulated around words like *Midwest, Illinois, prairie, Lincoln,* and *Chicago,* most of it not even written down, mountains that can barely be suggested by the handful of texts we have looked at.

I have assumed throughout that the meanings of words like *prairie, Lincoln,* and *Chicago* are not natural or inevitable but instead are constructed; they are not simple mirrors of reality but the product of complex intertwinings of hopes, anxieties, wishes, desires, and fears, bound to history, not transcending it. The meanings of the prairie, Lincoln, and Chicago have been generated out of a large, imponderable question: what sort of human life can we create in this place? The prairie, Lincoln, and Chicago have been such potent figures of Illinois because they have offered spaces to consider this question. The prairie is an almost inevitable image of such an inquiry; vast, empty, and enigmatic, it seemed like a blank page upon which a vision of American life could be inscribed. Lincoln, sphinx-like in his apparent resistance to definitive interpretation, has served as another instance of the American Other, his elusive character a space for the staging of conflicts over the nature of "Americanness." Chicago, simultaneously American dream and American nightmare, has offered similar challenges to interpretation; to read it correctly would be to resolve the many contradictions of the sort of culture America has evolved.

If the writing of Illinois sounds remarkably like the writing of America in its confrontations with new experiences and its attempts to place them in relation to history, we should not be surprised. Chicago, as Charlie Citrine reminds us, and the prairie and Lincoln as well, are, after all, "just the USA." But the writing of America has taken its own direction in the writing of Illinois, and it persists in taking its own course as writers continue to search for what sort of life a life in prairie land should be.

Works Cited

Addams, Jane. 1910. *Twenty Years at Hull-House*. With an introduction and notes by James Hurt. Prairie State Books. Urbana: University of Illinois Press, 1989.

Algren, Nelson. 1951. *Chicago: City on the Make*. New York: McGraw-Hill, 1983.

Amis, Martin. 1987. *The Moronic Inferno and Other Visits to America*. Harmondsworth, England: Penguin.

Angle, Paul M., ed. 1968. *Prairie State: Impressions of Illinois, 1673–1967, by Travelers and Other Observers*. Chicago: University of Chicago Press.

Basler, Roy P. 1935. *The Lincoln Legend: A Study in Changing Conceptions*. Boston: Houghton Mifflin.

———. 1985. "Lincoln and American Writers." *Papers of the Abraham Lincoln Association* 7:7–17.

Baxter, David J. 1983. "The Dilemma of Progress: Bryant's Continental Vision." In *William Cullen Bryant and His America,* ed. Stanley Brodwin and Michael D'Innocenzo. New York: AMS Press.

Bellow, Saul. 1944. *Dangling Man*. New York: Vanguard.

———. 1953. *The Adventures of Augie March*. New York: Viking.

———. 1964. *Herzog*. Viking Critical Library. New York: Viking, 1976.

———. 1968. "Looking for Mr. Green." In *Mosby's Memoirs and Other Stories*. New York: Viking.

———. 1975. *Humboldt's Gift*. New York: Avon, 1976.

———. 1982. *The Dean's December*. New York: Harper and Row.

Beveridge, Albert J. 1928. *Abraham Lincoln, 1809–1858*. 4 vols. Boston: Houghton Mifflin.

Bloom, Harold. 1984. Review of *Lincoln: A Novel,* by Gore Vidal. *New York Review of Books,* July 19, 5–8.

Boewe, Charles. 1962. *Prairie Albion: An English Settlement in Pioneer Illinois*. Carbondale: Southern Illinois University Press.

Bray, Robert C. 1982. *Rediscoveries: Literature and Place in Illinois*. Urbana: University of Illinois Press.

Bremer, Sidney. 1981. "Lost Continuities: Alternative Urban Visions in Chicago Novels, 1890–1915." *Soundings* 64:29–51.

———. 1984. "Willa Cather's Lost Chicago Sisters." In *Women Writers and the City,* ed. Susan Merrill Squier. Knoxville: University of Tennessee Press.

Brooks, Van Wyck. 1952. *The Confident Years, 1885–1915*. New York: E. P. Dutton.

———. 1954. *Scenes and Portraits*. New York: E. P. Dutton.

Bryant, William Cullen. 1914. *Poems*. Oxford Edition. Oxford: Oxford University Press.

Callahan, North. 1970. *Carl Sandburg: Lincoln of Our Literature*. New York: New York University Press.

Campbell, Roy. 1949. "A Veld Eclogue: The Pioneers." In *Collected Poems,* vol. 1. London: Bodley Head.

Chénetier, Marc. 1976. "Vachel Lindsay's American Mythocracy and Some Unpublished Sources." In *The Vision of This Land: Studies of Vachel Lindsay, Edgar Lee Masters, and Carl Sandburg,* ed. John E. Hallwas and Dennis J. Reader. Macomb: Western Illinois University.

Chernoff, Maxine. 1986. *Bop*. New York: Vintage.

Claridge, Henry. 1988. "Chicago: 'The Classical Center of American Materialism.'" In *The American City: Literary and Cultural Perspectives,* ed. Graham Clarke. London: Vision.

Clayton, John J. 1979. *Saul Bellow: In Defense of Man*. Rev. ed. Bloomington: Indiana University Press.

Cobbett, William. 1819. *A Year's Residence in the United States of America*. 2d ed. Carbondale: Southern Illinois University Press, 1964.

Colander, Pat. 1985. *Hugh Hefner's First Funeral and Other True Tales of Love and Death in Chicago*. Chicago: Contemporary Books.

Colter, Cyrus. 1970. *The Beach Umbrella*. Iowa City: University of Iowa Press.

Costello, Mark. 1973. "Murphy's Xmas." In *The Murphy Stories*. Urbana: University of Illinois Press.

Cox, James M. 1988. "Regionalism: A Diminished Thing." In *Columbia Literary History of the United States,* ed. Emory Elliott. New York: Columbia University Press.

Current, Richard N. 1986. "Fiction as History: A Review Essay." *Journal of Southern History* 52:77–90. Reprinted in Richard N. Current, *Arguing with Historians*. Middletown, Conn.: Wesleyan University Press, 1987.

Davis, Allen F. 1973. *American Heroine: The Life and Legend of Jane Addams.* New York: Oxford University Press.

Davis, Cullom. 1988. "Illinois." In *Heartland: Comparative Histories of the Midwestern States,* ed. James H. Madison. Bloomington: Indiana University Press.

DeVoto, Bernard. 1948. Editor's Note to *The Valley of Shadows* by Francis Grierson. New York: History Book Club.

Donald, David Herbert. 1948. *Lincoln's Herndon.* New York: Knopf.

Dondore, Dorothy Anne. 1926. *The Prairie and the Making of Middle America: Four Centuries of Description.* Cedar Rapids: Torch.

Douglas, Ann. 1977. "*Studs Lonigan* and the Failure of History in Mass Society: A Study in Claustrophobia." *American Quarterly* 26:487–505.

Duncan, Hugh D. 1965. *Culture and Democracy: The Struggle for Form in Society and Architecture in Chicago and the Middle West during the Life and Times of Louis Sullivan.* Totowa, N.J.: Bedminster.

Dybek, Stuart. 1990. *The Coast of Chicago.* New York: Knopf.

Edwards, Owen Dudley. 1985. "Fiction as History: On an Earlier President." *Encounter* 64:33–42.

Ellmann, Richard. 1973. "W. B. Yeats." In *Norton Anthology of Modern Poetry,* ed. Richard Ellmann and Robert O'Clair. New York: Norton.

Etter, Dave. 1987. *Selected Poems.* Peoria, Ill.: Spoon River Poetry Press.

Faragher, John Mack. 1986. *Sugar Creek: Life on the Illinois Prairie.* New Haven, Conn.: Yale University Press.

Farnham, Eliza W. 1846. *Life in Prairie Land.* With an introduction by John Hallwas. Prairie State Books. Urbana: University of Illinois Press, 1988.

Faux, William. 1823. *Memorable Days in America.* London: Simkin and Marshall.

Fehrenbacher, Don E. 1987. "The Fictional Lincoln." In *Lincoln in Text and Context: Collected Essays.* Stanford: Stanford University Press.

Flower, George. 1882. *History of the English Settlement in Edwards County, Illinois.* Reprinted. Ann Arbor: University Microfilms, 1968.

Fried, Lewis F. 1990. "James T. Farrell: The City as Society." In *Makers of the City.* Amherst: University of Massachusetts Press.

Frye, Northrop. 1957. *Anatomy of Criticism: Four Essays.* Princeton, N.J.: Princeton University Press.

Gibbons, Reginald, and Fred Shafer, eds. 1984. *Chicago. TriQuarterly* 60.

Grierson, Francis. 1909. *The Valley of Shadows: Sangamon Sketches.* With an introduction by Robert Bray. Prairie State Books. Urbana: University of Illinois Press, 1990.

Hallwas, John E. 1981–82. "Eliza Farnham's *Life in Prairie Land.*" *The Old Northwest* 7:136–45.

——— . 1984. "John Regan's *Emigrant's Guide:* A Neglected Literary Achievement." *Illinois Historical Journal* 77:269–94.

——— , ed. 1986. *Illinois Literature: The Nineteenth Century.* Macomb: Illinois Heritage Press.

Henderson, Harold. 1986. Review of *Chicago*, by Studs Terkel. *Illinois Times,* Dec. 11–17, 10–11.

Herndon, William Henry, and Jesse William Weik. 1889. *Herndon's Lincoln: The True Story of a Great Life.* Chicago: Belford, Clarke.

Hicken, Victor. 1976. "Sandburg and the Lincoln Biography: A Personal View." In *The Vision of This Land: Studies of Vachel Lindsay, Edgar Lee Masters, and Carl Sandburg,* ed. John E. Hallwas and Dennis J. Reader. Macomb: Western Illinois University.

Hoover, Paul. 1988. *Saigon, Illinois.* New York: Vintage.

Irwin, John T. 1980. *American Hieroglyphics: The Symbol of the Egyptian Hieroglyphics in the American Renaissance.* New Haven, Conn.: Yale University Press.

Johannsen, Robert W. 1989. "Sandburg and Lincoln: The Prairie Years." In *The Frontier, the Union, and Stephen A. Douglas.* Urbana: University of Illinois Press.

Jones, Alfred H. 1974. *Roosevelt's Image Brokers: Poets, Playwrights, and the Use of the Lincoln Symbol.* Port Washington, N.Y.: Kinnekat.

Kolodny, Annette. 1984. *The Land before Her: Fantasy and Experience of the American Frontiers, 1630–1860.* Chapel Hill: University of North Carolina Press.

Lindsay, Vachel. 1925. *Collected Poems.* New York: Macmillan.

——— . 1979. *Letters of Vachel Lindsay.* Ed. Marc Chénetier. New York: Burt Franklin.

——— . 1984–86. *The Poems of Vachel Lindsay, Complete and with Lindsay's Drawings.* Ed. Dennis Camp. 3 vols. Peoria, Ill.: Spoon River Poetry Press.

——— . 1988. *The Prose of Vachel Lindsay, Complete and with Lindsay's Drawings.* Ed. Dennis Camp. 2 vols. Peoria, Ill.: Spoon River Poetry Press.

McJunkin, Penelope Niven. 1982. "Seeing Sandburg Plain: The Search for Carl Sandburg." In *Selected Papers in Illinois History, 1981,* ed. Bruce C. Cody. Springfield: Illinois State Historical Society.

Maloff, Saul. 1974. Review of *The Last Carousel,* by Nelson Algren. *New Republic,* Jan. 19, 23–24.

Massa, Ann. 1970. *Vachel Lindsay: Fieldworker for the American Dream.* Bloomington: Indiana University Press.

Masters, Edgar Lee. 1916. *Spoon River Anthology.* New York: Macmillan.

——— . 1920. *Mitch Miller.* New York: Macmillan.

——— . 1922. *Children of the Market Place.* New York: Macmillan.

————. 1926. *Lee: A Dramatic Poem*. New York: Macmillan.

————. 1928. *Jack Kelso: A Dramatic Poem*. New York: Appleton.

————. 1931. *Lincoln: The Man*. New York: Dodd, Mead.

————. 1935. *Vachel Lindsay: A Poet in America*. New York: Scribner's.

————. 1936. *Across Spoon River: An Autobiography*. New York: Farrar and Rinehart.

Maxwell, William. 1980. *So Long, See You Tomorrow*. New York: Knopf.

Miller, Ross. 1990. *American Apocalypse: The Great Fire and the Myth of Chicago*. Chicago: University of Chicago Press.

Nelson, Cary. 1989. *Repression and Recovery: Modern American Poetry and the Politics of Cultural Memory, 1910–1945*. Madison: University of Wisconsin Press.

Newlin, Paul A. 1983. "*The Prairie* and 'The Prairies': Cooper's and Bryant's Views of Manifest Destiny." In *William Cullen Bryant and His America*, ed. Stanley Brodwin and Michael D'Innocenzo. New York: AMS Press.

Newman, Judie. 1984. *Saul Bellow and History*. London: Macmillan.

Oates, Stephen B. 1984. *Abraham Lincoln: The Man Behind the Myths*. New York: Harper and Row.

Olson, Steven Douglas. 1986. "The Metaphor of the Prairie in Nineteenth-Century American Poetry." Ph.D. dissertation, University of Illinois.

Powers, Richard. 1988. *Prisoner's Dilemma*. New York: William Morrow.

Randall, James G. 1936. "Has the Lincoln Theme Been Exhausted?" *American Historical Review* 41:270–94.

Regan, John. 1852. *The Emigrant's Guide to the Western States of America, or, Backwoods and Prairies*. 2d ed. Edinburgh: Oliver and Boyd.

Ringe, Donald A. 1954. "Kindred Spirits: Bryant and Cole." *American Quarterly* 6:233–44.

Ruggles, Eleanor. 1959. *The West-Going Heart: A Life of Vachel Lindsay*. New York: Norton.

Rusk, Ralph Leslie. 1925. *The Literature of the Middle Western Frontier*. 2 vols. New York: Columbia University Press.

Sandburg, Carl. 1926. *Abraham Lincoln: The Prairie Years*. 2 vols. New York: Harcourt Brace.

————. 1939. *Abraham Lincoln: The War Years*. 4 vols. New York: Harcourt Brace.

————. 1968. *The Letters of Carl Sandburg*. Ed. Herbert Mitgang. New York: Harcourt, Brace, and World.

————. 1970. *Complete Poems*. Rev. ed. New York: Harcourt Brace Jovanovich.

Sanford, Charles L. 1957. "The Concept of the Sublime in the Works of Thomas Cole and William Cullen Bryant." *American Literature* 28:434–48.

Silverberg, Robert. 1968. *Mound Builders of Ancient America: The Archae-ology of a Myth*. Greenwich, Conn.: New York Graphic Society.

Simonson, Harold P. 1966. *Francis Grierson*. New Haven, Conn.: College and University Press.

Smith, Carl S. 1984. *Chicago and the American Literary Imagination, 1880–1920*. Chicago: University of Chicago Press.

Spencer, Theodore. 1948. Introduction to *The Valley of Shadows* by Francis Grierson. New York: History Book Club.

Stern, Richard. 1987. "Chicago in Fiction." In *The Position of the Body*. Evanston, Ill.: Northwestern University Press.

Terkel, Studs. 1986. *Chicago*. New York: Pantheon.

Thacker, Robert. 1989. *The Great Prairie Fact and Literary Imagination*. Albuquerque: University of New Mexico Press.

Thomas, Benjamin P. 1947. *Portrait for Posterity: Lincoln and His Biogra-phers*. New Brunswick, N.J.: Rutgers University Press.

Thomson, Gladys Scott. 1953. *A Pioneer Family: The Birkbecks in Illinois*. London: Jonathan Cape.

Thwaites, Reuben Gold. 1906. Preface to *Memorable Days in America* by William Faux. In *Early Western Travels, 1748–1846*, vol. 11, ed. Reuben Gold Thwaites. Cleveland: Arthur H. Clark.

Vidal, Gore. 1984. *Lincoln: A Novel*. New York: Ballantine, 1985.

———. 1988. "Gore Vidal's *Lincoln*? An Exchange." *New York Review of Books*, Apr. 28, 56–58.

White, Hayden. 1973. *Metahistory: The Historical Imagination in Nineteenth-Century Europe*. Baltimore: Johns Hopkins University Press.

———. 1978. *Tropics of Discourse: Essays in Cultural Criticism*. Baltimore: Johns Hopkins University Press.

Will, George F. 1989. "How Reagan Changed America." *Newsweek*, Jan. 9, 13–17.

Williams, Kenny J. 1981. *Prairie Voices: A Literary History of Chicago from the Frontier to 1893*. Nashville: Townsend.

Wilson, Edmund. 1962. *Patriotic Gore: Studies in the Literature of the Ameri-can Civil War*. New York: Oxford University Press.

Woodward, C. Vann. 1988. Reply to Gore Vidal. *New York Review of Books*, Apr. 28, 58.

Wrenn, John H., and Margaret M. Wrenn. 1983. *Edgar Lee Masters*. Boston: Twayne.

Index

Note on the Author

JAMES HURT, a native of Kentucky, has taught since 1966 in the English department at the University of Illinois at Urbana-Champaign. A specialist in modern English, Irish, and American literature, he has written *Catiline's Dream: An Essay on Ibsen's Plays,* many articles on drama, modern literature, and Illinois literature, and several plays, including *Abraham Lincoln Walks at Midnight,* which was produced each summer from 1980 to 1987 at New Salem State Park.